The Unwins Book of Sweet Peas

The Unwins Book of
Sweet Peas

Colin Hambidge

Silent Books
Cambridge

Thanks to John Bishop of the National Sweet Pea Society for his invaluable assistance.

Drawings on pages 23, 24, 25, 29, 35, 38, 43, 44, 45 and 46 by Kathryn Ball
Drawings on pages 70, 77, 78 and 80 by Paul Margiotta
Frontispiece: 'Colin Unwin'

First published in Great Britain in 1996
by Silent Books Ltd
Swavesey, Cambridge CB4 5QG
for Unwins Seeds Ltd

ISBN 1 85183 095 2

British Library Cataloguing-in-Publication Data.
A catalogue record of this book is available
from the British Library

Printed in Hong Kong by Midas Printing Ltd

Contents

Preface

It was back in 1926, seventy years ago, that Charles Unwin first published his *Sweet Peas, their History, Development and Culture*, a work which was to become one of the great textbooks on the subject. The late "Mr Charles" was one of the world's leading authorities on the subject for most of his lifetime, devoting himself to hybridising new varieties and becoming totally immersed in his great floral love. It was a pleasure and a privilege to be asked to write *The Unwins Book of Sweet Peas*, which incorporates the knowledge built up at Unwins over nearly a century. I hope that what follows will be of interest to keen growers and newcomers alike.

My aim has been to present easy-to-follow cultural methods whether sweet peas are to be grown by the beginner or the already enthusi-astic gardener who may be considering exhibiting blooms at a local show. Also included is a background to the sweet pea and some historical notes, along with a section on the basics of hybridising, a pursuit which can give endless pleasure to the enthusiast. It is a delight to work so close to the country's favourite flower, and to gain some insight into its nature and development by watching the company breed and introduce so many new varieties. The sweet pea is rightly called "The Queen of the Annuals", for what other flower can match its elegance, beauty, perfume and ease of culture?

COLIN HAMBIDGE
Histon
Cambridge
1996

Sweet peas for quick, easy, sure-fire blooms

Welcome to the world of sweet peas, one of the best-loved flowers in the world. Whilst this volume has been written for enthusiast and beginner alike, may I assume for one moment the reader has never before grown a sweet pea, but would like to do so with the minimum fuss and bother, the aim being to provide plenty of fresh flowers for cutting?

Just follow these simple steps and you are virtually guaranteed to be cutting your own beautiful sweet peas in just a few weeks.

I At any time from late January to early March, sow five to seven seeds per 12cm (5in) pot of all-purpose seed and potting compost. Cover the seeds with 1cm (0.5in) of compost, water well, then place the pots in an unheated greenhouse.

2 Do not water again until the seedlings emerge, usually about 6 to 14 days after sowing. Then water regularly to ensure the compost never dries out.

3 Once the seedlings have developed two pairs of leaves, pinch out the growing tip to encourage side shoots to grow, thereby giving good, bushy plants.

4 In early March, fork over a strip of garden about 1m (3ft) wide, removing weeds and breaking down clods until soil becomes fine and crumbly to the feel.

5 Insert a row of 2.4m (8ft) bamboo canes across the strip you have prepared at intervals of about 45cm (18in) to a depth of about 30cm (1ft).

6 Attach some pea and bean nylon netting (available from garden centres), twine or string to the canes to make a framework for the plants to climb.

7 From mid March to mid April, plant the seedlings singly at intervals of 20cm (8in) along the supports, taking great care not to damage the roots as you separate the young plants. A few strands of black cotton or short twigs placed close by will help protect against sparrows.

8 As the seedlings grow, water them if dry weather prevails, and encourage them to grow up your frame by lightly tying the stem to the netting or string.

9 The first flowers will probably appear around mid June, but the later you sow, the later the plants will flower.
THE GOLDEN RULE As soon as the plants start to flower, cut the blooms for the house, and do not leave them on the plants because they will produce seed and your plants will stop flowering. The more you cut the flowers, the more you will get.

10 Place the cut blooms in a vase, and await gasps of admiration on your gardening prowess from family and friends.

Yes, growing sweet peas really is as easy as that, and do not let anyone tell you otherwise.

Tempted to try? We hope so! For a little more information, please read on...

Classification of sweet pea types

Spencer

The classic sweet pea descended from the sport of Eckford's Prima Donna which was named Countess Spencer. The Spencers have a wonderful colour range, long stems, varying degrees of perfume and are the most highly prized by exhibitors of the flower. They usually have four blooms per stem, which can all be open at the same time.

Galaxy

Multi-flowered types which can carry up to eight, and sometimes more, blooms per stem. They flower at much the same time as the Spencers and possess a good range of colours.

Early Multiflora Giganteas

Popular with the cut flower trade, these flower earlier than the Spencers, producing large, good-quality blooms well placed on firm stems. The Mammoth Series flower at the same time, and generally are a longer-stemmed and bigger-flowered improvement.

Cuthbertson

Also known as Cuthbertson Floribundas, they were named after Frank Cuthbertson of the Ferry-Morse Seed Company, USA. They are the result of crosses between Spencers and an early-flowering American type. Flowering around a fortnight earlier than the Spencers and able to withstand high early summer temperatures better, they generally produce between four and six blooms per stem, although the range of colours is more limited than that of the Spencers. The Royals were also introduced by Ferry-Morse, and may be seen as an improvement on the Cuthbertson, being longer– and stronger-stemmed and with greater vigour and flower size.

The Unwins Stripes/new Heavenly Series

The Unwins Mixed Stripes, also known as

Super Snoop

Butterfly Mixed, offer an extensive range of colours including crimson, scarlet, orange-scarlet, blue, salmon-rose, lilac, chocolate and purple. The flowers are marked, veined and picoteed on cream or white grounds, and the overall impression is of the petals having been lightly flecked with spots of paint. An improvement on flower size and quality came in 1991, when Unwins introduced Candy, with flowers of silver-grey with a picotee rim, flecked with chestnut-maroon. But now the Stripes story has moved on yet another stage, with the introduction of a completely new race of sweet peas bred and introduced by Unwins — the Heavenly Series — a vast improvement on the original Unwins stripes. The first two varieties in the series, Mars and Nimbus, were introduced for 1996 and others are in the pipeline. The Heavenly Series are far superior in flower size and form to the old Stripes, and have a stunning flecked appearance. They were on public display for the first time at the 1995 Hampton Court International Flower Show where they attracted great attention from many visitors.

Hammett Bicolors

Bred in New Zealand by Dr Keith Hammett, these striking and unusual bicolors include pale pink on carmine, pink on rose, violet on blue and white on lavender. They usually produce four or five blooms per stem, and are particularly attractive when seen as a cut flower.

Unwins Stripes

Patio mixed

Intermediates

Over the years, many crosses have been made between the tall Spencers and dwarf types in attempts to produce low-growing intermediate (or semi-dwarf) types. Much of the breeding work has been undertaken by American companies, who have come up with some good series.

The Bijous grow to around 45cm (18in) high in a good range of colours. They need very little support other than a few short sticks and look effective in beds, borders or even large containers. Their relatively long stems mean they can also be used for cutting if required. Better stem length is achieved, however, by growing some of the newer, taller intermediates such as the Knee-Hi, Jet Set or Continental series, which tend to grow to around a metre (3ft) high. All may be supported or left to "do their own thing". All have good vigour and colour range.

Acacia Leaved Types

These are unusual sweet peas which do not produce tendrils, but have in their place narrow "acacia-like" leaves arranged in the shape of a rosette. These are natural mutations. There are three intermediate types generally available – Snoopea, which grows to around 60cm (2ft) and Supersnoop, bred from Snoopea, having longer stems and flowering a little earlier. The more recent Explorer is con-sidered to be a further improvement of this type. Because of their spreading habit, they are a good means of providing some unusual ground cover.

The Dwarfs

Dwarf sweet peas, those which grow to between 15 and 30cm (6 – 12in) really have little more than curiosity value and have never been widely grown. The Patio series is available in a good range of colours and is compact in growth, while the Cupids are predominantly pinks and have a more lax growth habit. Their short stems mean they are not suitable for cutting, but they are worth considering for edging beds, borders or even growing in pots and hanging baskets.

Fantasia is a new mixture, which is fragrant, free-flowering, and includes not only many colours, but bicolors and other intriguing shades.

3

Species of Sweet Peas

The name "Lathyrus" was used by Theophrastus, from the Ancient Greek name for the pea, combining *la* (very) and *thoures* (a stimulant), as the seeds were said to have irritant properties.

The Lathyrus genus consists of more than 150 species, with our own sweet pea being *Lathyrus odoratus* (the only one to be scented) and the perennial sweet pea *Lathyrus latifolius*. Whilst it is not possible to discuss them all within this brief chapter, it is interesting to consider a few of the more garden-worthy species.

The earliest to flower is *Lathyrus vernus* or spring pea, which can flower as early as mid-March. It is a herbaceous perennial, which grows to a height of 40cm (16in), and looks very good at the front of a border. Each stem bears up to eight mauve-purple blooms. Plants are usually trouble-free, and clumps increase steadily with the years.

Back with the annual, climbing types, *Lathyrus chloranthus, chrysanthus,* and *tingitanus* are three worth growing. *L. chloranthus* produces small, narrow, lime-green flowers, which contrast well with the rich rose-pink blooms of *L. tingitanus,* or Tangier Pea. *L. chrysanthus* usually grows no higher than 60cm (2ft) and is often plagued with greenfly, but is notable for its golden yellow flowers so sought by the hybridists.

Lathyrus nervosus, also known as Lord Anson's blue pea, is a perennial and native of South America. Growing to around 180cm (6ft), it produces whorls of small indigo flowers. *L. sativus,* the Indian Pea, is an annual which only grows to around half the height. *L. sativus* bears its flowers singly, however, and they have white standards with blue central blotches and wings. Its clear blue form, *L. sativus* "Azureus" is sometimes confused with *L. nervosus.*

Lathyrus latifolius, the perennial or everlasting sweet pea, is a great favourite for cottage gardens, where it lasts for years.

Sweet pea Charles Unwin

4

Early Days — The Monk and the Minister

The sweet pea is one of the best examples in horticulture of a species which has changed and developed rapidly in a relatively short space of time, thanks in part due to the constant work of the hybridist and in part to the hand of Nature. As we know it today, the flower bears scant resemblance to its forebears of two centuries ago.

A plant with a Sicilian habit

It was certainly unheard of in England until the end of the seventeenth century, and the earliest mention of the sweet pea in a botanical work appears in 1700. It is generally believed the first sweet pea seeds appeared in England in 1699, having been sent to the Enfield, Middlesex, schoolmaster Dr Robert Uvedale by Franciscus Cupani, a monk living on the island of Sicily.

Those Sicilian sweet peas from which Cupani harvested the seed to send to Dr Uvedale probably originated on Malta, when we consider the sweet pea still grows wild there, whilst there are no records of its having been found in its wild state in Sicily.

Whilst we do not know for sure the colour of those first sweet peas, they were probably all the same shade — most likely a bicolor with a maroon-purple standard and magenta-purple wings, for this is a throwback which still occasionally occurs in crosses today. What is certain is that the flowers would have been very small in comparison with those of today — little larger than those of a culinary pea — borne in twos or, at best, threes, and on much shorter stems. Equally as certain is that this sweet pea was sweetly and heavily perfumed, and very free-flowering. It is easy to see from such a description that the flower would have had only limited appeal either as a garden subject or cut flower.

Little is heard of the sweet pea again for a century or so, although we know its popularity began to spread during the eighteenth century as it was offered commercially by 1750. By 1800 there were five varieties now known - for in addition to the purple bicolor there was a white, a maroon, a red and a pink and white bicolor, the so-called Painted Lady which had appeared as early as 1726. How these four new varieties came into being is unclear. Maybe they too were imported from Sicily, Malta or elsewhere, and there is always the possibility they came about as the result of natural cross-fertilisation. But, judged on how the sweet pea has behaved in later years, the most likely explanation is that these variations cropped up quite naturally and haphazardly as mutations or "sports" from the original maroon-purple. Even with a range of five colours, it has to be said that the sweet pea remained an unprepossessing subject, and it received scant attention from gardeners and florists alike.

Henry Eckford - Father of the Sweet Pea

We must now take another great leap in time from 1800 to the mid to late 1880s, and to a man who probably did more than anyone before or since to improve and popularise the little sweet pea — Henry Eckford of Wem in Shropshire, remembered affectionately as "The Father of the Sweet Pea", and still revered in the small town where he settled and conducted his work. Eckford was a Scot who had earlier worked on improving calceolarias, cinerarias and verbenas before turning his attention to the sweet pea.

It is unlikely that Eckford himself realised the full potential which the flower possessed at the outset of his hybridisation work, but we may be sure he had a clear idea of what he wanted to achieve. In a relatively short time, by cross-fertilisation and meticulous selection, he altered the very structure of the flower, eliminating some of its poorer points, making it larger and bolder and introducing a wider

Painted Lady

range of colours. Equally as important, he left unimpaired its good points – its daintiness, perfume, freedom of flowering and vigour. His work on sweet peas brought Henry Eckford widespread and international acclaim.

Interest in sweet peas, and in Eckford's new varieties or "novelties" in particular, grew rapidly. Special classes at flower shows were soon devised for sweet peas, where once they would only have been shown amongst collections of annuals.

Demand for sweet peas as cut flowers also grew, and by the turn of the century William Unwin of Histon was growing large numbers of sweet peas on the edge of the Cambridgeshire fens to supply the demand from London's Covent Garden and other flower markets.

The flower's popularity was surely sealed in 1901 when a small band of sweet pea enthusiasts founded the National Sweet Pea Society, an organisation which has played a huge part in the flower's development and which continues to thrive. The Society has through its trials, exhibitions, publications and conferences done much to stimulate, maintain and develop interest in its flower.

The sweet pea offered those Victorian gardeners two great advantages – it responded well to good methods of cultivation and it was not greatly bothered by pests and diseases – two factors which helped to establish its popularity. Once Eckford showed what the sweet pea was capable of, others began to turn their hand to hybridisation. Such was the activity and development associated with the sweet pea

that it might have been reasonable to believe that by the beginning of the twentieth century it had reached the pinnacle of its development.

At this stage in the sweet pea's development, it is worth considering its flower form and parts. Its flower comprises the calyx, the tiny leaves which protect the petals while they are still in bud, the standard or upright back petal, the two wings which spread apart just beneath the standard, and in between them the keel, which is really two petals joined in the shape of a narrow boat-like sheath. The keel has the important role of covering and pro-

William Unwin

Cut flower production

tecting the fertilising organs of the flower and the undeveloped seed pod.

The sweet peas which Henry Eckford developed in the late nineteenth century were generally larger flowered than the much smaller blooms produced by the original Sicilian and its four sports. For this reason, Eckford's varieties were termed "grandifloras". The standards of these grandifloras varied from variety to variety. Some were shell-shaped or almost hooded while others were flat and open, just like a culinary pea, sometimes with a notch in the top and occasionally with two notches.

The Countess and the Seed Company

And so it was that at the beginning of the twentieth century the sweet pea was a beautiful flower but one which was marking time. It was then that Nature played her great hand in the game and astounded the sweet pea world with her dexterity and ingenuity. Truly it was the stuff of which horticultural dreams are made when an event only a little short of a miracle occurred in one summer in three distinct locations throughout England.

One evening during the summer of 1901 William Unwin was showing two fellow choristers round his rows of sweet peas after choir practice when he noticed something strange in the variety Prima Donna, a popular pink variety raised by Henry Eckford. Prima Donna was fairly large-flowered, had a slightly hooded standard, was a vigorous grower and produced plenty of four-bloomed sprays. What was particularly remarkable to William was that some of the blooms had much larger standards than usual and these standards were rather waved or frilled. In addition, the wings were longer and larger and the keel had also changed to become larger, wider and considerably looser knit near its end. This came to be known as the "open" keel rather than the "clamped" keel.

This represented a major alteration of form, brought about by mutation or sporting, and William Unwin was swift to realise the importance of this lucky occurrence. And he was not alone! At Althorp Park in nearby Northamptonshire, home of the Earl Spencer, head gardener Silas Cole noticed a very similar sport among his plants of Prima Donna. Silas saved his own selection, and named and introduced it as Countess Spencer.

From this name the term "Spencer type" was derived, the first of the modern race of sweet peas we still grow and exhibit today. We also know that a similar mutation appeared appropriately enough in Henry Eckford's own Prima Donna plants in Wem, although we do not know what became of this selection.

The Histon selection which William Unwin saved was introduced under the name Gladys Unwin, and subsequently proved to be a little different from Countess Spencer in that the flowers were not quite as large or as wavy. Gladys Unwin would have been more accurately described as an intermediate type, being halfway between a Spencer and a grandiflora. Varieties developed from it, such as Frank Dolby and Nora Unwin, were given the separate name of "Unwin type" to differentiate them from the Spencers.

While the Unwin varieties were true to type and colour, many of the early Spencers were unfixed. Indeed, it was said that Countess Spencer was introduced a little too hurriedly. Nevertheless, in spite of this instability, the larger, wavier form of the Spencers soon outstripped the Unwin types in popularity. Before long the Unwin types had disappeared, surviving only in the pedigrees of some of the better Spencers.

The popularity of these Unwin types may have been short-lived, but it lasted long enough for William Unwin to introduce many new varieties, having turned his attention to hybridisation from cut flower production. By 1903 he had issued his first modest seed list which was eagerly sought by sweet pea enthusiasts, and in so doing he established the company which today is Unwins Seeds, still recognised for its breeding and introduction of sweet peas and still based in the village of Histon on the outskirts of Cambridge. By the beginning of the First World War, William Unwin was operating as a general seedsman, and had been joined in the business by his son Charles, a man whose name was to be even more closely linked to the sweet pea than was that of his father.

In the early years of the twentieth century, it soon became apparent that it was not difficult to hybridise sweet peas and to transfer the desirable flower size and frilliness of form to many colours. As a result a cavalcade of new Spencer types appeared in the pages of the seedsmen's catalogues.

Such was the interest in sweet peas that in 1911 the Daily Mail offered the huge sum of £1000 to the grower of the best bunch of sweet peas. The judging took place at the Crystal Palace in London, where some 38,000 bunches of blooms were entered. The prize was won by a minister and his wife from the Scottish borders. The competition did much to capture the public imagination and further increased the popularity of the flower.

William Unwin was understandably delighted to receive a letter from the winner of the £1000 stating "the plants I grow are mainly from your seed".

The Spencer type has been developed and refined throughout the twentieth century as new varieties are introduced annually. There have been other developments such as tendril-free, knee-high and "striped" sweet peas, but nothing on the scale of what happened in the summer of 1901. We are still seeking that elusive yellow sweet pea. It has been a long while coming, but who knows what the next hundred years may hold for the sweet pea?

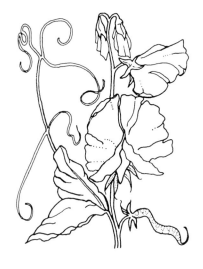

5

Sowing and care of seedlings

There are two main sowing periods for sweet peas, autumn (usually September/October) and "spring" (usually January/February), when seed is sown in pots in a cold frame or greenhouse. As sweet peas are hardy annuals, they may also be sown direct in their flowering position during the true spring of March and April.

While it is generally agreed by growers that the strongest plants and finest flowers are produced from an autumn sowing, and this is the practice of most exhibitors, excellent results can be achieved from a spring sowing. It is worth recalling the words of Charles Unwin, speaking in the first wireless talk on sweet peas from the London studio of the BBC on 16 October 1923.

"So much has been written and said on the subject of sweet pea culture that I am convinced many would-be growers are scared away, for they imagine the flower a difficult one to grow. The simple facts of the matter are these: the sweet pea is one of the very easiest, most adaptable, and most reasonable flowers we have, and can be successfully grown by anyone. Don't be frightened by elaborate cultural instructions, for if you can grow eating peas or runner beans, you can grow sweet peas. Almost any soil will be found suitable for obtaining a wealth of good blooms for garden and house decoration, even if only dug over and no more

Sowing seeds

Placing pots into a cold frame

time or money spent on it than on any ordinary flower or vegetable crop. Not the least of the virtues of the sweet pea is its ready response to good culture; it is the flower for the million, and to the ordinary flower-lover, with little time and facility for intensive culture, it affords greater results in proportion to the care bestowed upon it than any other flower in existence."

These comments are as valid today as they were then, and will hopefully encourage anyone to try growing sweet peas for the first time. As the ideal culture for growing autumn- or spring-sown plants differs, it is worth looking separately at the two seasons.

Autumn sowing

October is the main month for autumn sowing, but the actual time depends on localised weather conditions. As a general rule of thumb, growers in the north of England sow in late September while those in the midlands and south tend to favour the first two weeks of October. In the far north and Scotland, many growers rely on a January or February sowing.

Compost

Many keen sweet pea growers prepare their own favourite medium in which to sow, and these are well worth considering. A home-made mixture of four parts loam, one part sand and one part peat thoroughly mixed makes a first-rate compost and is easy to prepare. If it is not feasible or convenient to do this, sowings are best made in John Innes *seed* compost, which is readily available from garden centres and many other retailers. John Innes No. 1 potting compost also gives good results. Nowadays, many gardeners prefer to use one of the host of multi-purpose coir-based or peat-based seed and potting composts, which are widely available. I have had good results from proprietary brands including J. Arthur Bowers and Levington. It may be worth experimenting with a few different composts to see which performs best in your oughly two days before sowing and allow it to drain. Dry peat can take a long while to absorb moisture.

Which pots are best to use?

Traditional old-fashioned clay pots are not always easy to find nowadays and are usually more expensive than the much more common plastic pots, but there is no doubt they have many advantages for the sweet pea grower. It is worth taking a little trouble in tracking some down as they will last for years if well looked after.

Clay pots are porous whereas plastic pots are not, and this porosity is wonderful for encouraging healthy root growth. It also allows the compost to drain more freely following heavy rain. If clay pots are unavailable, do not be deterred as I have produced

Sweet peas in plastic pots, ready for planting out

conditions. There are no hard and fast rules, for experience counts for more than anything.

To determine how much compost you require, remember that an 80 litre bag of compost will fill more than thirty 12cm (5in) pots.

Whether using John Innes, a multi-purpose or a home-made compost, it is important to make sure it is moist yet crumbly at the time of sowing. Ideally, water the compost thor-

excellent plants from sowings made in plastic pots. But do avoid peat and fibre pots which then disintegrate in the soil. They are fine for spring sowings, when their use is short-term, but are not really suitable for autumn work.

Whether using clay or plastic pots, 12cm (5in) ones are the best size, sowing between five and seven seeds per pot evenly spaced at at a depth of 1–1.5cm (a half to three-quarters of an inch). Most clay pots have a single drainage hole in the bottom, and this is best "crocked" with a piece of broken pot or small flat stone slightly larger than the hole to aid drainage, but to prevent compost loss. Alternatively, seed can be sown in a seed tray at a spacing of 5cm (2in) between seeds. Lightly sift compost over the seeds to the required depth and gently tap it down with another pot, taking care not to compact the compost. Water lightly using a watering can with a fine rose after sowing and then, to retain moisture, cover the pots or trays with glass or polythene for a few days until the seedlings just begin to break the surface of the compost. It is vital to remove the covering as soon as the seeds begin to germinate.

Sweet peas growing in a cold frame

The benefits of a cold frame

There is no real substitute for a cold frame if you wish to produce the very best plants from an autumn sowing. There are many types and sizes available from garden centres or specialist mail order companies, and whilst they are seldom cheap they will usually last for several years. For the do-it-yourself enthusiast, it is not difficult to build a good wooden structure, or even one made from bricks. After all, a cold frame is really only four sides and a glass or perspex top.

Whilst it is possible to make autumn sowings in an unheated greenhouse, seedlings tend to grow far too rapidly and become leggy and unmanageable, whereas the beauty of a cold frame is that it enables the young plants to be grown "hard", by having the glass top off for most of the time, only needing to replace it when severe weather threatens. The plants grow slowly, and have the best start in life, whereas the temperature will fluctuate much more in an unheated greenhouse. If you are intending to use a greenhouse, however, it is a good idea to delay the sowing by about three weeks compared with a sowing destined for the cold frame.

Pots are best placed into the cold frame immediately after sowing. To help insulate the roots in autumn-sown pots, some gardeners fill the gaps between pots in the frame with peat, soil or weathered ash, but this is not necessary.

As soon as the seedlings emerge, remove the glass top (or "frame light") completely, and only replace it when the weather becomes very wet or when a hard frost threatens. Germination time is governed by a number of factors, but generally seedlings will begin to appear about six to fourteen days after sowing. Light frosts will not normally harm young sweet pea plants. During a hard, prolonged frost, some additional protection will be desirable, and it is worth placing old carpeting, matting, sacking or tarpaulin over the glass top.

The golden rule of sweet pea growing is: never attempt to remove this additional frost protection until you are sure the compost in the pots has thawed completely.

It will not harm the plants at all if the carpet or sacking remains over the frame day and night even for many days. A slow, steady thaw is imperative if the seedlings are to survive, but they will not be able to withstand the sudden thaw of being exposed to bright sunshine and heat.

If you are putting the top over just to protect against very heavy rain, allow some ventilation by allowing the back or front to be propped open.

In the time just after sowing and in the early stages of growth, mice can be a nuisance by eating the seeds, and small birds, especially sparrows, can cause havoc. Some strands of black cotton stretched over the frame can often prevent damage by birds.

Can germination be improved?

Much has been written on the subject of improving the germination rate of sweet pea seeds, and we hear of chipping the seed, soaking the seed, chipping and soaking, using seed dressing. Many sweet pea growers liked to coat their seeds in a powdered chemical seed dressing just prior to sowing, but at the time of writing (1996) such dressings are no longer available to gardeners.

All this adds to the myth that sweet peas are somehow a difficult flower to grow, but the truth is that most sweet pea seed will germinate perfectly readily with no extra "assistance".

But as with all rules, there are a few exceptions. Sweet peas vary in colour, size and the texture of their seed coat in the different varieties. The seed coats of some of the mottled and black-seeded varieties are hard and somewhat impervious to water, and careful "chipping" can sometimes aid germination.

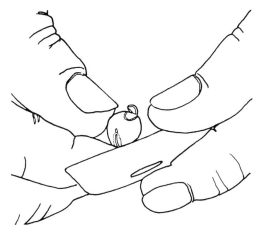

Chipping a seed to aid germination

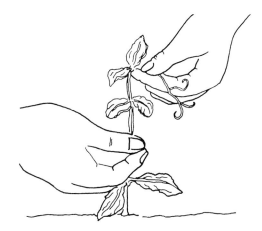

Pinching out – important in spring sowing

"Chipping" simply means the removal of a very small part of the seed coat with a small, sharp knife, taking care to avoid the "eye" or scar on the seed. But if all this sounds rather fiddly, let me assure you that chipping is by no means essential. Some sweet pea growers soak these mottled and black-seeded types overnight in water and then chip the few which have not swollen just before sowing. Research in the Unwins laboratory has shown that soaking sweet peas can cause stress and actually prevent germination, and we therefore strongly advise against soaking in water.

White, brown and wrinkle-seeded varieties should never be chipped. A few varieties are "soft-seeded" and behave in exactly the opposite way to those which are hard-seeded. Their seed coats are usually light chocolate in colour. Unfortunately, they have a tendency to rot before or during germination, especially if soil conditions are a little too wet or cold. With these soft-seeded varieties, germination rates can be improved by the addition of extra peat and sand to the sowing medium.

It is also a good idea to place a thin layer of sand in the pots and to sow the seed direct onto it. This will add drainage and prevent any waterlogging. It is a good general rule to use moist compost in which to sow, to water immediately after sowing and to refrain from watering again until the seedlings emerge.

Growing on the young plants

Once the seedlings emerge and until they are ready for planting out the following spring, they need very little attention to get through the winter. Do not attempt to pamper or "mollycoddle" them, but, instead, grow them slowly, hardily and sturdily. Remember also that too much water at their roots will do them much more harm than hard frosts. The sweet pea is naturally hardy, but it can sometimes be fussed into becoming tender.

Exhibitors often re-pot their seedlings singly into 7cm (3in) pots or special sweet pea "tubes", which allow good, deep root development. They use the same compost mixture as they did for sowing. This re-potting is usually done at any time between November and January whilst the weather is favourable. The very best time to do this is immediately before the first leaves begin to unfurl, when the seedlings are about 5cm (2in) high. This enables the young plant to be planted out to its final position with the root-ball intact and no disturbance to its roots – particularly advantageous if your soil is heavy. But this re-potting is certainly not essential, and most growers keep the seedlings growing on in their original pots until it is time to plant out.

In Unwins experience, the young plants can be left to grow away on their own, for they tend to "break" naturally (develop side shoots) without the need to be pinched out. With spring-sown plants, however, it is vital to pinch out.

Do not be tempted to feed or fertilise sweet pea seedlings, and take care not to overwater. As a general guideline, the young plants will only need watering if they are in danger of drying out. If the top of the frame is removed for most of the autumn and winter, the plants will usually receive enough moisture from the rains.

Spring sowing

By "spring" sowing, sweet pea growers generally mean January or February. The technique is very similar to that for autumn sowing, and it has to be said that spring sowing is very useful for those gardeners who do not want to care for plants from October onwards.

Similarly, it is convenient for those people who grow in the north of England or in Scotland, or who wish to show their blooms in late shows. Perhaps most importantly of all, spring-sown plants grow away with the days as they lengthen and are nearly always easy to manage. Bear in mind that as a general rule, spring-sown plants will flower about three weeks later than autumn-sown ones.

Sowings can be made in John Innes seed compost, John Innes No. 1 *potting* compost or a coir-based or peat-based multi-purpose seed and potting compost. As in the autumn, sow five to seven seeds per 12cm (5in) pot.

During January and February, temperatures in the cold frame will probably be too low for germination, and so until the seeds do germinate it is best to keep the pots "indoors", which may mean a spare room in the house, a frost-free shed or an unheated or heated greenhouse. At this period, it is vital not to get the seeds or germinating seedlings too wet, and so after the initial watering following sowing, do

A beautiful basket of Spencer sweet peas.

not water the compost again until the seedlings appear. This will help to prevent "damping off" in the soil.

As soon as germination has taken place, it is important to give the seedlings as much light as possible. The best place for this is the cold frame or the greenhouse. If using a cold frame, keep the top on for a few days until all the seedlings have emerged.

These spring-sown seedlings benefit from a little extra care in their early stages of growth because weather conditions are so often unfavourable, but, once established in the cold frame, the top may be left off during the day and all the time during any mild spells.

The importance of pinching out

What is more important for spring-sown seedlings is the need to pinch out their growing tips at a very early stage. Ideally this should be done immediately after the second pair of leaves has opened in order to encourage side shoots to develop as quickly as possible. If blooms are required for late (August) shows, it is, however, best to delay the stopping until four pairs of leaves have formed.

Equally as important for these seedlings is their need to be watered more often than those produced in the autumn. As sunshine and warmth increase during the lengthening spring days, it is vital to ensure the plants do not dry out. Give the plants a good drench when required.

If you do not have either a cold frame or a greenhouse, spring-sown seedlings can be brought along under cloches, ideally made of glass, although these are scarce and expensive nowadays. Polythene or perspex versions are generally more feasible and considerably cheaper. Allow air to circulate and offer the same protection as for plants in a cold frame, and good results are quite easy to achieve.

"True" spring sowing

The second type of spring sowing, which was touched upon briefly earlier, may be termed "true" spring sowing, and is perfectly acceptable if bunches of sweet peas are required solely for indoor or garden decoration. Seed may be sown direct in the flowering position, usually during March, although it is better to be guided by prevailing weather conditions than the calendar. Wait until the soil is beginning to warm up and becomes crumbly when rubbed through the hands. Sow the seed at about 2.5cm (1in) deep, and allow about 10cm (4in) between seeds.

Germination rates are unlikely to be as high from sowings made in the open as those made "under glass", and for economic reasons it is better to use the relatively inexpensive mixtures of seed available than the choicest varieties on offer from specialist seedsmen.

Ensure these sowings are well-watered if dry weather prevails, and as the seedlings emerge they will benefit from protection against birds. Black cotton is often a successful deterrent to sparrows, who seem to regard succulent sweet pea shoots as a delicacy.

To the gardener new to sweet peas, all this

may seem like a lot of bother to grow a few flowers, but in practice it is actually easy and straightforward – much of it being a matter of simple gardening and common sense. If you have never grown sweet peas before, do try them, for you will be captivated by them in a very short time.

6

Preparation of the soil

Sweet peas will flower well in a wide range of soil types and environments, and most garden soils will be capable of producing impressive blooms. They have the advantage, however, of responding remarkably well to above-average conditions, and if the following soil preparation and care is practised then quite spectacular results are perfectly possible.

Choosing the best site

The best place in the garden for the sweet pea plot is an open, sunny position where there is a good depth of topsoil and where you know from experience other flower or vegetable crops do well. It is a definite advantage if the area receives some shelter from east and north winds, and is reasonably well drained. If at all possible, run the rows from north to south so that both sides of the row receive their fair share of sunshine. An open, light, airy position encourages the development of sturdy plant growth and high-quality blooms.

A double row of sweet peas is often grown by many gardeners. For this purpose, the soil needs to be prepared to a depth of around 45cm (18in), and in strips about 120cm (4ft) wide. When preparing the soil for sweet peas, or any other crop, it is vital not to interfere with its natural layers. The topsoil must be left at the top and the subsoil must be left underneath. All digging and soil preparation should be completed by the turn of the year, the earlier the better, for this will give the plants the firm, settled root-run they love and in which they thrive.

Single- and double-digging

Excellent, well-balanced flower spikes are achievable from soil which has only been prepared to the depth of one "spit", a spit being equivalent to the length of the blade of the spade the gardener is using for the digging. Most keen growers tend to work their soil to a depth of two spits, while the ultra-keen will be prepared to work the soil to a depth of a metre or so!

This digging to a depth of two spits is really just double-digging, adding whatever

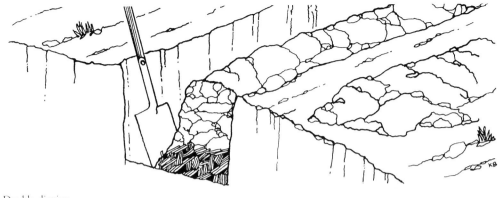

Double-digging

Single-digging

manure and fertiliser you wish as you go. The method may be to throw the top spit to one side and break up the lower spit where it lies, or to use the "step" method, throwing the top spit forward.

Strips 120cm (4ft) wide will suffice if your soil is light and well-drained, but if the soil is heavy or slow to drain, it is worth double-digging the entire site, even if you decide to limit the manuring just to the areas where the strips will be. It is best to break up large clods as you come across them, but leave the surface quite rough until the spring.

Can sweet peas be grown on the same piece of ground year after year? There is no hard and fast answer to this question, as so much depends on the type of soil, the nourishment it receives and the experience of the individual. There is no doubt that sweet peas can be grown successfully on the same land for many years, especially if it is medium to heavy, has not been over-manured and drains well, but

Trial grounds being manured in winter

unless you are already an experienced sweet pea grower, it is better to reverse the positions of the rows and the paths every year or two as a simple form of rotation.

The sweet pea grows relatively quickly and luxuriantly, producing new growth and flowers over a long period. It has a naturally extensive and wide-searching root system. We therefore need to provide not only the facility for it to develop freely, but also sufficient food at the time it is most needed. It is not easy to say what manure should be used and in what quantity, for much depends on the fertility and general state of the soil. But one thing is certain — over-manuring is much worse than under-manuring.

The value of manure

I still favour the incorporation of well-rotted farmyard manure, be it from cattle, horses, pigs or sheep, but it is becoming increasingly difficult to obtain nowadays, particularly in certain parts of the country. Alternatively, well-made compost can be used mixed with the manure or on its own.

Whilst well-rotted farmyard manure is bulky and often scarce, there are now several concentrated organic manures, derived from droppings, available from mail order companies and garden centres. These are hygienically packed, lightweight to move and economical in use.

On an "average", fairly well-drained soil which has not received any manure for two or three years, as you move and work the second or lower spit, mix in about a wheelbarrow load of manure to every 3 metre length of it. At the same time, mix in plenty of bone meal at the rate of three or four handfuls per square metre throughout the whole working, including the top spit. Bone meal is a good source of phosphorus, which stimulates the root development of the plants. The word "mix" is important here, for manures or fertilisers should never be placed in layers, sandwich fashion. A good dressing of dried natural seaweed fertiliser is also good and, like bone meal, perfectly safe to use.

If you use the same piece of ground for sweet peas the following year, cut down the amounts of manure and fertiliser by about a third, and in any following years by about a half. This should help prevent over-feeding the soil and keep it well balanced.

Once the site has been dug over, leave it to benefit from the effects of wintering, for frost, snow and rain action will help break down its structure to a fine, crumbly consistency or "tilth".

Liming

Before liming your soil, it is advisable to check the pH (alkalinity/acidity) of your soil to see whether this is necessary. Inexpensive soil-testing kits are readily available and simple to use.

If necessary, broadcast a moderate amount of hydrated lime over the surface of the soil during January or February. This will help reduce the acidity which is sometimes present in richer soils, while the calcium it provides is beneficial to the plants. If the soil has already been limed in the last year or two, do not lime again, but simply apply a dressing of a general-purpose garden fertiliser two to three weeks before planting out. If the ground is in really good heart, then neither lime nor fertiliser is really necessary.

When weather and soil conditions allow in the new year, fork over the surface once or twice, breaking up any remaining clods and working the top few inches of soil into a fine condition. Do not be frightened to tread about well as you do this, for this will help to settle the ground and provide a firm rooting medium.

Heavy soils

If you are intending to grow your sweet peas on heavy soil, it may be worth applying sulphate of potash to the top spit and basic slag throughout in place of bone meal to help improve matters. Try also to improve the physical structure of the soil by working in sand, peat or leaf mould, all of which will make the soil more open and easier for it to breathe. Ideally, give heavier soils their final forking over when they are beginning to dry out again after a wet spell — not always easy to time exactly, but well worth it if possible.

It bears repeating, however, that excellent blooms will still be produced from most garden soils which have been worked to the depth of just one spit with the incorporation of a well-balanced general-purpose fertiliser.

7

Growing on, care and feeding

Autumn-sown plants will of course be bigger and stronger than spring-sown ones, and will therefore be able to be planted out to their flowering positions earlier. Whilst it is more important to be guided by weather conditions than the calendar, try to plant out towards the middle or end of March. Aim for a day which is both dry and reasonably mild, and ensure there is no trace of frost in the soil.

The soil should be moist, but not sodden, preferably drying and nicely crumbly to the touch. If you are in any doubt as to the suitability of the weather or the soil, then wait a few days until you are happier with the conditions.

Supporting the plants

Shortly before planting out, you will need to prepare and erect the supports you are intending to give the plants. Exhibitors generally use 8ft bamboo canes, but the main object is to try and build a sound structure which will be able to withstand summer gales and carry the weight of the plants in full bloom. A framework of

posts and (with double rows) cross pieces of wood with stout strands of wire connecting them is one of the best

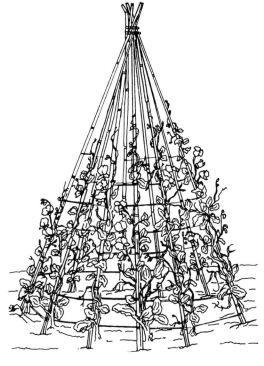

Wigwam-type support – ideal where space is limited

A well-developed root ball

Planting out in spring

ways of offering the canes support. The canes can then be secured to the wires just prior to planting out. Make sure the wooden cross pieces are just a little shorter than the width of the double rows so the canes can slope inwards a little.

If, on the other hand, you are not interested in growing blooms of the finest quality, but just want plenty of bunches of fragrant blooms for cutting, much simpler supports are quite adequate. A double row of tall canes forming an arch and draped with plastic netting, bushy pea sticks or just wire and string stretched between a few stout posts have all given good sweet peas in the past. If space is limited, a wigwam-type arrangement of canes is ideal and looks attractive. The sructure is usually very strong. And even if you are unable to supply any of these, sweet peas will always scramble up a chain link fence or wooden trellis with just a little encouragement.

Planting out and aftercare

Once the canes or other supports are in place, you are ready to begin planting. By March, all autumn-sown plants should be well and truly hardened off, and should receive very little check when set out. Aim to allow 20cm (8in) between plants. Plant at the front or the side of the canes. Where you have several plants in a 12cm (5in) pot, gently free the root ball from the pot and then carefully knead the ball with the hands. The soil can

Checking for good root development

Ensure that the prepared hole is large enough to accommodate the roots

be shaken away and the roots disentangled, all with the greatest of care to minimise damage and disturbance. Treat plants raised in seed trays or boxes in the same way.

If you re-potted the seedlings individually earlier in the season, loosen or untwine the coil of roots at the bottom of the pot, but otherwise plant with the soil ball intact, keeping the point where the first "break" or side shoot emerges on a level with the surface of the soil. Whilst you are in the process of planting out, it pays to keep the exposed roots covered with a damp cloth to prevent them drying out, especially if it is a particularly mild or windy day.

Using a hand trowel, make a hole large enough to take the roots of each plant spread out. Always plant firmly, and bed the plants in well with your hand or the handle of the trowel. It is good practice to draw up a little soil around the plants to prevent them blowing about and becoming loose. A few twigs placed in front of the newly planted seedlings will help protect them from winds and pests, and encourage them to grow away safely. Better still, lightweight perspex, corrugated tin lengths or sacking stretched between low posts will offer superb protection for two or three weeks after planting out. These may admittedly look a little unsightly, but they are only a temporary measure, and are well worth the trouble.

There is usually no need to water in plantings made in March, as soil conditions at this time of year are generally moist enough. Slugs too will need to be guarded against. There are now many different types of bait and trap available, some more environmentally friendly than others, but the choice is yours. Do not be tempted to delay taking precautions against

Firming plants in

make good root growth, which is the foundation of the flowering to be expected in the coming months.

Spring-sown plants will not usually be ready for planting out until six weeks or so after autumn-sown ones — mid-April to mid-May in general — but the planting technique is exactly the same.

Do not be deterred by sharp frosts after planting out, as these will not generally harm the plants if they have been hardily grown. Frost may mark the foliage a little, but no lasting harm should result.

birds and slugs for a day or two, as I know from painful experience that both can set to work within hours of planting out!

A useful tip when planting out is never to plant a seedling which has a brown "collar" on the white part of the stem above the seed, for within a few weeks these nearly always collapse suddenly and die. If you are planting out individually potted seedlings, remember to scrape away a little of the compost from the stem to make sure that a brown collar is not being concealed below soil level.

Relax!

Having planted these autumn-sown plants, it is now important to do nothing for a few weeks! Leave them well alone for at least four weeks and preferably six weeks. They may not look as if they are growing a great deal during this period, but they will be continuing to

A note on cordon versus natural growing

Up until now, the sowing, soil preparation and general care of the sweet pea plants has been virtually the same whether the grower is a keen exhibitor showing at national level or a keen gardener who likes nothing more than a house full of sweet peas throughout the summer. After planting out, however, the methods of growing part dramatically. The exhibitor's aim is to produce flower stems of the highest quality and size, and this involves a much more labour-intensive programme than that required to produce acceptable bunches of sweet peas for the vase in the dining room or kitchen.

If you are not intending to exhibit or do

not require blooms of the finest quality, all you really have to do is to let the plants "do their own thing" by scrambling rapidly up their supports. You may help them by loosely tying them in to prevent them flopping too much, but they will require little attention. The most important task to remember is that as soon as they begin flowering, you should cut the blooms continually, daily if necessary, to encourage further blooms to form. Flowers which are left uncut on the plant will form seed pods, and prevent further blooms from forming, thereby drastically reducing the flowering season.

Feeding

Sweet peas should not be fed or watered until they are well in flower. It is far better to rely on the good foundation which autumn digging and manuring will have provided. If feeding is necessary, try the old-fashioned but proven liquid manure and soot water, made by suspending a sack or bag containing farmyard manure and soot in a bucket of water for a few days, then dilute this "stock" with more water until it is about the colour of a light ale.

If you do not have the time or stomach for this, a general-purpose fertiliser, liquid or granular, may be useful, but err on the cautious side, and feed at rather less than the manufacturer's suggested rate.

The best method of liquid feeding is through the spout of a watering can into shallow drills drawn with a hoe about 20cm (8in) from the plants. Feeding once a fortnight is generally ample. Exceeding this dosage Charles Unwin compared rather graphically to giving a baby a beefsteak and thereby ruining the digestion!

8

Growing for showing

Restricting growth

Having allowed the young plants to settle in to their permanent positions for several weeks, they will need to have their growth restricted when they reach a height of 25–30cm (10–12in). On each plant, the strongest "leader" or growing point should be selected, and the remaining side shoots carefully removed with a knife or scissors. Then tie this leader loosely to its cane, but leave enough room for the stem or "haulm" to thicken as the plant develops. Raffia may be used for this purpose, but wire rings are quicker and easier to use. They should be at least 2.5cm (1in) in diameter.

You should then notice fairly rapid growth from the plant. From now onwards all tendrils (the means by which it naturally attaches itself to supports) and side shoots, which will form in every leaf axil, should be removed regularly when tiny with finger and thumb. The term "cordon" comes from these restrictive operations.

Whilst this can be a rather time-consuming task through the growing season, it is not difficult to learn. In fact, it is no more difficult than side-shooting tomatoes in a greenhouse,

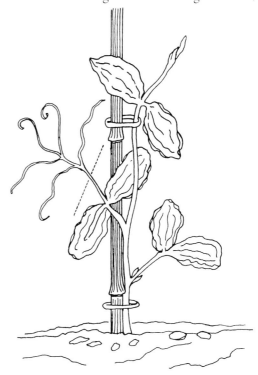

Take off tendrils and side shoots

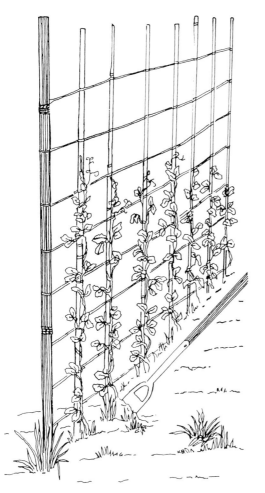

leaves, stems and flowers – will become much larger than if the plant had been allowed to develop totally naturally.

Quality versus quantity

The emphasis is on quality rather than quantity – a lower number of flowers, but larger and of finer quality is the exhibitor's or enthusiast's aim. The first few flowers on cordon-grown plants should not be allowed to bloom to allow them to build up strength. Simply pinch them out whilst they are tiny, and wait until little stems appear with four buds before they are permitted to bloom.

Some varieties are more vigorous than others, and with these it may be better if two leaders are allowed to develop, although both of these leaders should be grown up the same cane. If you are new to cordon growing, keep to just one leader until you have noted the behaviour of a number of varieties in your particular environment.

Hoeing regularly is an important part of the routine management of the plants, as this conserves moisture and keeps weeds in check before they have time to get established. But do not hoe too deeply. If your soil is on the light side or if the season is hot and dry, a mulch of short, well-rotted manure or even peat placed around the plants is useful for keeping the roots cool and moist. Mulching has the advantage also of doing away with the need for hoeing, and exhibitors often mulch in May or early June every year as a matter of routine.

so once again do not be deterred by the prospect if you are already a sweet pea grower and are considering cordon culture for the first time.

All we are actually doing is restricting growth above ground to one main stem, while at the same time encouraging as extensive a root system as possible below the ground. Not surprisingly, all the growth above the ground –

Lowering or layering

Tying up and pinching out side shoots and tendrils will need to be done about twice a week, and blooms will need to be cut regularly as they would be if being grown naturally. If the faded blooms are allowed to remain on the plant and the seeds are allowed to develop, the flowering season will be dramatically reduced.

Lowering or layering?

Plants grown on the cordon method are capable of growing much taller than those raised by the natural bush method. So what happens as the growing tips approach the top of the canes? Growers usually drop or lower their plants to allow them to continue flowering. In the sweet pea world, this process is generally known, rather misleadingly, as "layering", which to most other gardeners is a form of propagation.

When the plants reach a height of between 120 and 180cm (4–6ft), they are gently lowered, laid along the ground and then re-trained up a cane further along the row.

Begin the operation at one end of an outside row by unfastening all the ties on the first four to six plants and laying them out on the ground at an angle to the row, so they are less liable to damage. Then, taking great care not to break the haulm, lay the next plant along the ground close up to the canes and gently bend its top 30–40cm (12–16in) up to the first cane in the row, fastening this top part with two or three raffia ties. Remember that this top 30cm (12in) or so of the sweet pea plant can be very brittle and therefore easily snapped off.

The results of layering

Make a gradual rather than a sharp or "hairpin" bend lower down the haulm, starting it at ground level. Then the next plant is fastened likewise to the second cane, and so on until the end of the row is reached.

The first few plants in the next row are then brought round to take the places of the last plants of the previous row, and the first plants of the first row then go into position on the last canes of the second row.

This may all sound complicated and something of a contortionist's trick, but it is surprisingly easy in practice. The beginner may be frightened of breaking the haulm, but once the first few plants have been handled successfully, then confidence will inevitably grow.

It is generally believed that it is better to drop the plants during a spell of dry weather rather than wet weather, as the haulms are less inclined to crack. Having said that, it is a good idea to give the plants a spray with water once the dropping has been completed. Once the operation is over, the plants will generally be at a height of around 30cm (1ft). For the sake of neatness, it is good to keep the plants at the same height as each other.

A quicker way of layering (lowering)

If you are not bothered by being without blooms for around a fortnight, there is a quicker and easier method of "layering". First, remove all the flower buds, then unfasten all the ties on the plants, and lay them close up to the canes as already described. After a few days, the heads of the plants will have started

Preparing for a show

to grow upwards naturally, and they can then be tied to the nearest available cane.

This method has the added advantage of giving the plants a worthwhile break from flowering, and eliminating the risk of breaking the haulm.

This lowering or "layering" process can be performed once or twice in a season, if necessary. Far from distressing or harming the plants, it tends to improve the quality of subsequent blooms.

Some exhibitors actually layer their plants before they begin flowering, for this can coincide with the first shows. Layering causes bent stems to be produced for around a fortnight, and can therefore become inconvenient if the necessity to layer clashes with the approach of a particular show.

Preparing for an exhibition

An entire volume could easily be written on the subject of exhibiting sweet peas, and even then the matter would not have been exhausted. I shall attempt to cover what I consider to be the essential points as fully but as briefly as I can.

First, the blooms must be cut so that they will be at their peak at the hour of judging – perhaps an obvious statement, but one which bears repeating. They must arrive at the show undamaged and staged in a manner which enhances their good points.

Cutting for a show is best done early in the morning on the day before the show. This allows the blooms at least 24 hours to "fill out" in water. Cut those blooms which have the top bud a little more than half-open,

Charlie's Angel – highly prized by exhibitors

although prevailing weather conditions may force you to cut at a slightly earlier or later stage.

Whether you leave them in a cool, shady spot in water after cutting to "keep them back" or place them in a warm, light place such as a greenhouse to "bring them on" again depends on the weather and the stage at which they have been cut.

The blooms are best cut on a dry day, but this is not always possible. If you do have to cut them after a heavy dew or rain has left the petals wet, immediately after cutting take them in handfuls of around 18 spikes, hold them firmly at the base of their stems and, with a downward movement of the hand "swish" as much water off them as possible. Then stand the spikes somewhere under cover where they can be in a strong draught to dry off. If you are unable to find a sufficiently draughty spot, you could consider using an electric fan.

Getting to the show

Never pack blooms for showing while they are still wet or even damp. After wiping the stems quite dry with a cloth, lay the spikes flat in layers in ordinary cardboard boxes of the type used by florists. The stems themselves can be protected with greaseproof paper, as any trace of moisture is liable to mark the petals. During transit, make sure that they are secure and cannot be shaken about or in any way bruised.

On arrival at the show, the first job must be to get the stems back into water, loosely spreading out the heads of the spikes as you do so. The usual aid to the arrangement of the spikes in the vase is to fill it fairly tightly with thin rushes, these being cut off level with the brim. The sweet pea is essentially a light, graceful flower which is seen to best advantage in the show vase if given adequate space and not overcrowded.

Select only the very best spikes – those which are likely to be at their best when the judges examine them.

What are the judges looking for?

In its recommendations to its judges the National Sweet Pea Society (NSPS) suggests the following five criteria be taken into account:

i   Freshness, cleanliness and condition
ii   Form, placement and uniformity
iii Trueness of colour
iv   Size of bloom in balance with stem
v   Presentation

Let us examine these five points a little more closely:

i Freshness counts heavily, so see that the bottom bloom on every spike has not started to droop. If necessary, it is better to use a spike where the top bloom is not fully open than one where the bottom bloom is tired. Blooms should be blemish-free, with no trace of aphids or caterpillars.

ii "Form" means good form. Malformed flowers, those with some of their petals out of proportion or not quite in the correct place, are to be avoided. The placement of the blooms on the stem should be even, and not gappy. Over-watering, over-feeding and unbalanced feeding are three of the main causes of such gappiness. Bad placement can actually be rectified fairly quickly. If the stems become too long and the blooms too gappy, stop pinching out side shoots until a better balance returns to the blooms. On the other hand, feed and water if the stems are too short and the blooms become too bunched. Four well-poised, forward-facing florets alternately spaced at regular intervals is the aim.

iii Regarding trueness of colour: if, for example, a vase of the lavender variety Daphne is staged, it will probably be disqualified if in addition to Daphne a spike or spikes of another lavender variety is included. If the show schedule states "one variety" or "six varieties", this stipulation must be followed exactly. In fact, there should be no variation due to virus, scorch, refrigeration, excessive use of covers or additives after cutting.

iv Balance. Here it may be best to quote direct from the NSPS guidelines: "Size of bloom should be representative of the cultivar without coarseness, and uniform throughout the vase. Stems should be straight with length and texture proportionate to size of bloom, without weakness in the neck, coarseness or flattening".

v Effective presentation has a decided bearing on the four preceding factors, and it has to be said that experience and close observation of what other exhibitors are doing will help considerably. Presentation involves not only the arrangement of the spikes within the vase, but also the arrangement of the vases themselves. Count the spikes again in each vase before leaving your exhibit, and fill each vase to the brim with water just prior to the beginning of the judging.

After judging, note carefully why the exhibit has failed (unless it won!), and if you still feel unsure why this has happened, do not be afraid to ask the judge.

NSPS judges use the following pointing system:

Freshness, cleanliness and condition	7pts
Form, placement and uniformity	6pts
Trueness of colour	4pts
Size of bloom in balance with stem	3 pts
TOTAL	20 pts

Points are not awarded for presentation, but it should be assessed prior to pointing. If exhibits are judged to be of equal merit, preference will then be given to the better or best presented exhibit.

Which varieties are best for showing?

So which are the best sweet peas for exhibition? The Spencer is undoubtedly the best type at present because all the other types have features which are considered detrimental from a showbench standpoint. While some varieties of Spencers are better than others for exhibition, there is no such thing as the best ten or top twenty. Ask any twelve successful exhibitors what is their idea of the best twelve varieties, and it is highly unlikely that any two will choose the same dozen varieties.

In deciding which varieties to grow initially, it is best to stick to the well-tried, popular and reliable exhibition varieties. Varieties which are the most popular for showing are somewhat limited in number and colour range. Some are not popular with ordinary sweet pea growers. Exhibitors tend to avoid some colours altogether. Grow only one or two varieties more than you actually need. When deciding on varieties, vary the colours as much as possible, and avoid growing any two varieties with the same or very similar colouring.

A very useful guide exists in the Audit of Varieties of sweet peas exhibited at the National Sweet Pea Society's shows which, each year, gives the total number of vases exhibited of each variety, together with the prizes won. It is an excellent guide to the comparative popularity of exhibition varieties, and is included in the Society's Annual.

Nowadays an increasingly large number of keen sweet pea exhibitors give their plants some form of overhead protection, usually by means of an open-sided polythene structure, which is invaluable for preventing rain damage to delicate blooms. The structures can be either permanent or mobile, and are best made of thin-grade polythene to allow as much light as possible through to the plants. Exhibitors can usually do without such protection in most seasons, and it has to be said that polythene covers tend to make the blooms lose a little of the intensity of their true colours.

9

Fashions, trends and the future of the sweet pea

It is probably reasonable to assume that the public desire for new varieties of all species of flowers will continue in the coming years. In simple economic terms, a packet of new sweet pea seeds is cheap compared with the price one has to pay for a new orchid, or even a new rose. This appears even better value when one considers the years of development and selection which have gone before the seed is filled into the packet.

Apart from the arrival of Countess Spencer and Gladys Unwin back in the very early days of the twentieth century, change in sweet peas has been so gradual that it is easy to forget the very great differences which exist between our modern varieties and those of Eckford. Who is to say we

Mars

shall not experience another similar "quantum leap" at some time in the future which advances the sweet pea considerably beyond what we know of it at present?

Whilst none of us can be certain, I believe the sweet pea still has a great capacity for improvement and change, and that we are not yet at the zenith of its development. For instance, there are still many desirable shades and colours not found in the species, especially the highly prized yellow! There has been no real deepening in cream sweet peas since the time of the grandiflora The Hon. Mrs Kenyon, so surely one is due before too long?

There are also possibilities with bicolors, stripes, picotees and flushes. The new Heavenly series presently being introduced by Unwins is the latest development, and a major advance on the older "striped" varieties. Their flower size and form are a great improvement on what went before, and the colour combinations are particularly eye-catching.

Much has been written about the perfume of sweet peas, and the seeming loss of fragrance amongst modern strains. It may be a case of a fonder remembrance of things past, when everything was somehow better, but scent has perhaps declined a little ever since the arrival of the Spencers. Almost all modern varieties are fragrant to some degree, and this fragrance always seems stronger under warm, dry conditions than in cool, wet weather. But sweet peas with a strong scent are undoubtedly still being bred and introduced to gardeners.

Lightness is one of the

Galaxy Mixed

flower's greatest attributes, and it is a little difficult to imagine how a change of form could improve upon this. Both exhibitor and gardener alike love a large flower, and an increase in flower size will always be considered desirable by them. But how far will flower size be able to grow before its lightness is jeopardised?

IO

A note on named varieties

In the course of this volume, the reader may have noticed that few sweet peas are referred to by name, but that rather colours and shades are used. The reason for this is that sweet peas are subject to fashion just as much as are cars or music or holiday destinations.

What is popular and widely grown today may have been forgotten in five years' time, especially if a new and improved strain has superseded it.

Many sweet peas have stood the test of time, and indeed become more popular as they age, and will continue to be grown for many years to come. Others fall by the wayside, usually because gardeners do not want to grow them and it is no longer worthwhile for the seedsmen to offer them.

If I was a betting man, which I am, and was forced to name those modern varieties which I believed would still be going strong ten or twenty years hence, I would choose the following varieties as my "Ten to Follow" from the Unwins range - Brian Clough, Jilly, Charlie's Angel, Mrs Bernard Jones, Daphne, Royal Wedding, Colin Unwin, Charles Unwin, Champagne Bubbles and The Doctor.

We shall see!

Sweet peas as cut flowers

Is there any flower better suited or more beautiful as a cut flower than the sweet pea? It has such a light, ethereal quality and so much natural grace that however displayed in a vase or arrangement it cannot fail to attract attention. And what better natural room freshener is there than its exquisite perfume, so unlike any other? I am biased, of course, but I know that many others share my view.

The colour range is extensive, and whilst not all colours of the spectrum are yet available in sweet peas, virtually all gardeners will find some shades to their taste. Take your pick from maroon, crimson, shades of orange, pink and cerise, mauve, lavender, all tones of blue, white, cream and a wide range of subtle colour combinations. Sweet pea growers use the term "ground" often, perhaps describing a variety's colour as "pink on a cream ground". All this means is that the variety has a cream background visible through the pink.

Her Majesty

Mixed floral arrangement

Learning from Nature

There is much to be said for studying Nature when arranging any kind of flowers, and sweet peas are no exception. Their flowers grow naturally gracefully, poised in the air around the plant almost like butterflies. If we observe these naturally grown, not cordon grown, plants they serve as a good model for what we can try and achieve in an indoor arrangement. Aim for enough blooms to make a worthwhile show of colour, but not so crowded that the only impression given is one of colour.

Exhibition-quality spikes with their long, stiff stems are of a more formal appearance than naturally grown blooms, and this makes them a little more difficult to use in light or dainty arrangements. They can, however, look effective in larger displays.

In many arrangements, you may want to bend the stems of some blooms to add interest and form. If you wish to give stems a more pronounced bend, take a normal, straight stem and pull it slowly through the first finger and thumb of the left hand, exerting fairly firm pressure, while at the same time gently bending it as required with the right hand. This is best done a few times, bending the stem just a little more each time.

When to cut?

So when is the best time to cut flowers for the house? Late evening and early morning are

The finishing touch to a mixed display

generally considered to be two of the best times, although there are no hard and fast rules. Use a sharp pair of scissors or a good penknife, ideally one kept just for cutting sweet peas. Cut blooms with as long a stem as possible – they can be shortened later if necessary. Place them in water immediately after cutting and, if possible, leave them "to have a drink" for a few hours.

Jilly

Extra life

There are several proprietary vase-life lengtheners available from florists, and these can be very effective. Most are in powder form and are simply mixed with water to form a solution. Unwins research has shown that the vase life of cut blooms can be improved significantly by the use of these preparations, and they are therefore well worth considering.

Some colours and particularly the more delicate shades tend to lose some richness if the

Sweet peas in a Latvian market place

sun has been shining on them for a few hours, although they improve after a while in water. When cutting for the vase, avoid those flowers which are fully open, as the bottom bloom will begin to droop in just a few hours. It is better to choose ones where the top bloom is still at the bud stage, or a little beyond.

Vases and companions

The choice of vase is, of course, a matter of personal preference, but slender, clear vases usually display blooms better than heavy or highly coloured ones. Plain glass and silverware are both excellent. Exhibition-type blooms are well suited to ornamental baskets in a hallway, fireplace or in the corner of a room.

Sweet pea foliage complements the flowers well in a vase, having shapely leaves and curly tendrils, and ornamental grasses or even pretty, wild grasses can look effective. But the traditional companion of the sweet pea as a cut flower is gypsophila, the light, tiny, white-flowered annual or perennial, which helps to create an even lighter appearance to the entire display. Asparagus ferns, particularly indoor types such as plumosus, also look good when combined with sweet peas.

A note on colours and light

The blending of colours and shades in any particular arrangement is a matter of personal taste, although some blend more harmoniously than others. White and lavender shades can help create a cool effect in a room, while cream and orange would give a markedly warmer feel.

Lighter shades tend to look at their best in daylight and seem to lose some of their delicate colouring under artificial light. The deeper colours, which may seem somewhat harsh in daylight, may improve under artificial light, especially if a few creams or whites are also included. Varieties with orange or salmon in their composition usually look very effective under light.

The following are suggestions of two-colour combinations which I believe look effective and pleasing:

• Cream or light cream-pink combined with orange, salmon, orange-scarlet, orange-cerise or lavender.

• White combined with virtually any colour or shade not on a cream "ground".

• Light blue or lavender combined with orange, salmon or salmon-cerise.

• Pale pink blushes or flushes on white grounds combined with light lavenders or lavender-blues.

If you wish to combine three colours, include just a few of the colour which is the most decided contrast to the other two, and keep these blooms towards the bottom of the arrangement. Try one of the following:

• White and pale pink combined with a few red, orange or maroon.

• Cream and light cream-pink combined with a few orange, salmon or cerise.

• Cream and salmon-cream-pink combined with a few orange or orange-scarlet.

Having said that, there are no rules, so why not experiment a little and devise your own favourite colour combinations. You are only limited by your imagination.

12

Growing in a cold greenhouse

Have you ever considered growing sweet peas in a greenhouse or polythene tunnel for beautiful early blooms of great quality? It is well worth a try, and can give some stunning flowers. Anyone who has seen blooms grown on the cordon system in an unheated greenhouse is certain to have been impressed by their clean, unsullied appearance and clear colours when compared with those grown outside exposed to the elements.

Advantages

Two of the great advantages of indoor culture are the relative freedom from disease such plants experience and the greater control over the

growing regime the gardener has. Polythene tunnels are relatively inexpensive nowadays, and after the initial expense of the purchase, running costs are virtually nil. While a larger garden is needed to accommodate such a structure, even a relatively small tunnel will be capable of producing first-

rate blooms.

This cold greenhouse culture actually varies little from standard outdoor culture, whether grown by the cordon method or by just growing them naturally. Early autumn sowing once again gives best results, although planting out should be done about a fort-

Young plants in a poly-tunnel

night earlier than if they were to be set outdoors.

Keep the young plants out in the cold frame until around the middle of January, and then bring the pots into the greenhouse. Greenhouse soil can soon become "tired", and it is sometimes advisable to remove some of the old, and bring in some new. At the same time, it is worth incorporating some well-rotted leaf mould or similar into it. There is no need for special trenching, and the same method of soil preparation should be followed as earlier described for outdoor culture.

Seedlings can be planted out during February, at a spacing of 10–15cm (4–6in) apart. Plant them firmly, and do not water too freely at first. Keep the soil just moist until the plants start to grow away strongly. Do make sure the young plants receive plenty of fresh air, and although they are under cover, still grow them as coolly as possible, and never try to force them with extra heat. Guard

also against sudden fluctuations in temperature by opening ventilators fully on warm days and closing them down towards evening.

Support

As the plants are unlikely to be buffeted by strong wind, their system of support need not be as substantial as that required for plants outdoors. Wide mesh netting is very good, even for cordon-grown plants, or stout string or twine tied vertically on two or three horizontal wires will work well. If vertical strings are being used, tie these loose-

ly to the horizontal wires so the plants can be twisted round them as they grow.

Once the plants begin to flower, light feeding with liquid manure is beneficial, and regular watering becomes very important. The foliage will benefit from occasional light sprayings of water, ideally brought up to the temperature within the greenhouse before being used.

Lower the plants when the tops reach the glass. This can be done as many as three times a season under glass. Plants grown in this way will often produce blooms continuously from April (depending

Tying-in plants in a poly-tunnel

on the season) until as late as early September.

Interestingly, some colours of sweet pea are much better under glass than others. Those varieties which need shading from the sun outdoors to keep their colour perform particularly well in a greenhouse or tunnel. Generally, all varieties which have salmon or orange in their make-up tend to improve under glass.

Cold green house culture

Sweet peas at Christmas?

And how about the ultimate in sweet pea growing – cut blooms for Christmas! It was certainly possible by sowing the Early Spencer or winter-flowering types from August to early September. Sadly, these strains are no longer readily available, although it looks likely that there may be some development in this area in the reasonably near future.

There is already a variety called Winter Elegance available which looks promising.

They did not require any artificial warmth, but needed to be kept frost-free. Blooming in about eighteen weeks from sowing, they never made as much growth as late types. It was best to sow in large pots in a cold frame, and then move them indoors without transplanting well before the winter sets in. Allow them to grow naturally, and do not pinch them. With a little luck, you may be able to go out to the greenhouse to cut a bunch for the Christmas dinner table.

13

Breeding new varieties

The science of genetics is complex, but some of its basic facts can be conveyed simply and in unscientific language to give an insight into how new varieties can be bred not only by horticultural companies but also by enthusiastic amateur hybridisers in their own gardens. To my mind, one of the great beauties that the sweet pea possesses is that it can be successfully hybridised in most fair-sized gardens because different varieties do not need to be isolated from each other.

Plants perpetuate themselves in several different ways, but here we are concerned solely with sweet peas, which do so by means of seed. Both male and female organs are present in each individual flower, and both are usually ready to function at the same time.

Male and female

The male organs are the stamens, which have little pollen sacs called anthers at their tips, and when these are ripe they burst and release the powdery pollen, which in most flowers is yellow in colour. The female part of the flower is housed in one or more pistils, the parts of which are the stigma, style and ovary. In a

Pollination

covered with fine hairs. The style leads to the ovary, which is the immature seed pod, containing the undeveloped seeds.

Sweet pea fertilisation is the same as with other flowers, pistil and stamens being ripe at the same time. The pollen is transferred by contact to the stigma and to the tiny hairs. The pollen grain then throws out a "tube" which pushes through the surface of the stigma, through the style, into the ovary, where it can fertilise one of the ovules or immature seeds.

In the case of the sweet pea, pollen gets on to the stigma by direct action. The sweet pea is rather unusual in that it naturally self-pollinates or self-fertilises, each flower using its own pollen for the purpose. The two petals which are joined to form the keel cover the pistil and stamens at the time of fertilisation. Further protection is given by the other petals, as fertilisation actually takes place before the flower is totally open. If you examine a number of buds just at the point of opening, you will see the exact point at which the anthers burst, and it will then be apparent that the flower is not liable to cross-pollination by wind or insects.

Pollination

Pollination

sweet pea, these can be revealed by stripping away the petals and the keel. The stamens will be seen surrounding the pistil. On closer scrutiny, the very end or stigma will be found to be sticky, while just underneath it will be

This self-pollination is a tremendous boon

to those growers who would like to try their hand at breeding new varieties. It means that a large number of different varieties can be grown side by side, as there is no possibility of accidental cross-fertilisation taking place and spoiling the trueness of seed stocks, as would be the case with most other flowers.

Cross-fertilisation

This is simply the fertilisation of one variety by the pollen of another. The artificial cross-fertilisation of any flower implies the removal of its own anthers before they shed their pollen, and the transfer of pollen from another variety to its pistil, taking care to ensure that no pollen from any other source can reach the pistil while it is still potent.

A bud on the point of opening is chosen. Hold it gently but firmly in the left hand (assuming you are right-handed). Fold back the standard and wing on the left side and hold in that position with fingers. With a small pair of tweezers or forceps, the keel is cut in two from top to bottom, thereby exposing the anthers and pistil. Take care not to injure the pistil in any way. You will be able to see at once whether the anthers have already burst and released their pollen. If so, begin again, this time choosing a slightly younger flower. Experience is quickly gained, and correct selection soon becomes easy.

All the stamens now have to be removed by the tweezers, and once more it is important not to puncture or otherwise damage the pistil. The flower which is to become the female parent has now been emasculated. Then choose a half-open bloom of the variety you have chosen as the male or pollen parent. Gently pull down the keel to reveal the stamens and pistil. It is then quite straightforward to transfer the ripe pollen on to the stigma of the female parent by contact, or by the aid of a small, fine-haired brush. One disadvantage with using a brush is that it must be thoroughly cleaned between crossings before the pollen of another variety can be used, and it is also rather wasteful of the pollen.

Theoretically, any buds of the right age on a sweet pea stem are equally suitable for crossing, but in practice it is perhaps best to make the first or oldest bud on any stem the female parent. It is sometimes possible to cross the first two buds on a stem at the same time. All other buds on the stem should now be nipped off, and a label attached to the stem stating the number of the cross. Always keep exact and thorough records of all plant breeding, and ensure these are kept safe year after year, for they will prove invaluable.

Unlike so many other flowers, with sweet peas there is no need to protect the female parent after cross-fertilisation with a paper bag or similar, as it is virtually unheard of for foreign pollen to upset the cross which has been made.

When to hybridise?

While the actual operation of crossing sweet peas is relatively simple, some judgement has to be used in deciding when best to make the crosses so that seed pods have every chance of

Bridget and Pat Richardson (*née* Unwin) with sweet pea Bridget

developing. A spell of fine, sunny weather in the first two or three weeks of July is about the right time for autumn-sown plants, while mid-July to mid-August is better for spring-sown plants. Autumn-sown plants nearly always provide the better seed crop, and the hybridist is really better off using only these ones. If early flowers are used for the purpose, they sometimes abort before seed pods mature.

There will be no obvious change in the condition of the blooms which have been artificially cross-fertilised. Granted good fortune, as the days and weeks progress seed pods should begin to form on the female parents.

Carefully gather the seeds when ripe, but before they are shed, and keep each cross separate and carefully numbered.

The F1 generation

The plants which will result from this cross-fertilised seed in the first generation are known as F1s, or the F1 generation. Usually the colour of the flowers of these F1s is the same, but different from either parent. So a cross between a white and a creamy-pink may give a red, maroon or purple in its F1 generation. It is only when you are dealing with a cross in

Norwich terrier and sweet peas

which one or both parents are unfixed or untrue that there will be any colour variation in the F1s. Always remember to hold back a little of your F1 seed, and do not use it all for the production of the F2s.

The F2 generation

The next or F2 generation is generally much more interesting, for this is when colour variations will occur. This is all very fine, but there are two very important questions which you may already be asking yourself:

1 How do you decide which varieties to choose as parents?
2 How do you select which of the F2 generation to keep and which to discard?

There is no easy answer to either of these questions, and it is only really through experience and determination that a grower can develop an eye for a potentially good new variety.

But the budding plant breeder does not have to rely on guesswork or make a host of random crosses in the hope of developing a worthwhile variety. It is impossible to foresee

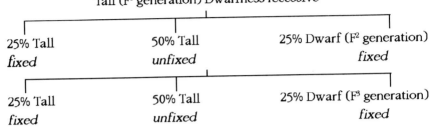

A CULINARY PEA CROSS

True Tall x True Dwarf (parents)

Tall (F^1 generation) Dwarfness recessive

| 25% Tall | 50% Tall | 25% Dwarf (F^2 generation) |
| fixed | unfixed | fixed |

| 25% Tall | 50% Tall | 25% Dwarf (F^3 generation) |
| fixed | unfixed | fixed |

A culinary sweet pea cross

the exact outcome of any crossing, but some knowledge of what is likely to happen can help give us some clear aims and objectives, and this can save many years of experiment.

We have come to realise, for instance, that to a certain extent like produces like, and that pure fixed stocks breed true. Translated to the canine world for a moment, we would not expect two pure-bred Norwich terriers to produce anything other than Norwich terriers. The breed's characteristics are handed down intact from generation to generation, barely changing over the years. We can only bring about major changes in hereditary characteristics by hybridisation.

This gives us considerable scope for activity, but there are also some fairly basic limitations. On the whole, crosses can only be carried out between varieties of the same species,

occasionally between varieties of the same genus but different species, and only rarely between varieties of a different genus.

The basics of sweet pea breeding

No mention of any plant breeding could pass without mention of Gregor Mendel, a priest born in 1822, who through his research established many of the principles we now know as genetics. He found, by crossing varieties of plants or animals of the same species but with markedly different characteristics, that fixed laws governed the extent and ratio in which those characteristics were inherited by progeny.

Some of his most famous work was conducted on culinary peas, close relations of course to our own sweet peas. As an example, let us take two varieties of pea, each with an opposite characteristic, in this instance tallness and dwarfness. Assuming both varieties are fixed or true, we might reasonably expect that when crossed the first or F1 generation would consist of plants of a height about halfway between that of their parents. We would, however, actually find that all the plants were tall, and there would be no evidence to suggest one parent was dwarf.

Mendel found somewhat similar behaviour in other crosses of plants with opposite characteristics. The particular character which emerged almost intact in the F1 generation he termed "dominant" for obvious reasons, while the character which remained submerged in the first generation he called "recessive". It is not possible to find such a distinctive degree of dominance in every cross made, but in hybridising plants we do find that virtually all hereditary pairs of opposite characteristics can be classified as dominant or recessive, although the degree of dominance may vary.

What would happen to seed saved from this F1 generation of culinary pea? We would find, as Mendel did, that the recessive factor, dwarfness, would re-assert itself in about a quarter of the plants produced. If these plants are then carried forward from this F2 generation into a third, fourth and fifth generation, we would find they remain perfectly true to this dwarfness and give no indication that one

of the parents of the original cross was tall.

But what about the remaining 75 per cent of tall plants in the F2 generation? Though these were all tall, we would discover, if we saved seed fom them, that only one-third would remain true to tallness in future generations, whilst the other two-thirds (that is 50 per cent of the total F2 generation) would again, in the F3 generation, split up in the same proportion as did the F2s, namely one-quarter true dwarfs, one-quarter true talls, and one-half untrue and unfixed talls.

The illustration on page 70 will make this rather involved explanation clear and, once grasped, the important basic principle of genetics will be mastered.

The matter does become rather more involved when we try to deal with more than one pair of opposite characteristics in the same cross. Staying with culinary peas a moment longer, if we cross a tall, late variety with light green foliage, large pods, wrinkled seeds and good flavour with a dwarf, early pea which has dark green foliage, small pods, round seeds and poor flavour, then we have six pairs of opposite characteristics, which can combine with each other in many clear-cut and different ways. In practice, differences may not be clear-cut, and intermediate stages in height, size of pod, flavour or foliage colour may multiply almost indefinitely the possible variations. Put another way, it is usually necessary to raise a large number of plants of the F2 generation to be sure of bringing out in most crosses their full range of variations or permutations.

The plant breeder's objective

The objective of the plant breeder is essentially to combine in one plant two or more desirable characteristics found in two separate varieties. He may take an early, heavy-cropping pea of poor flavour and cross it with a late variety of good flavour, the objective being to produce an early, heavy-cropping pea with a good flavour. Coming back to sweet peas, there have always been some varieties which have had excellent size of bloom, and one of the main objectives of breeders has been to combine that size with other colours.

The bringing together of two desirable characteristics in one plant is not always an easy matter! In the FI generation they are combined and in a way reduced to a state of flux, but in the F2 generation, they do not always behave how we would hope. Some may link up, but some may never do so. Certain characteristics are sometimes reluctant to fuse together. One only has to look at human beings where dark hair is usually associated with dark eyes, while fair hair is only very rarely associated with dark eyes.

The most exciting time for the potential sweet pea breeder is surely when the F2 generation of plants begin to flower, for this is when the crosses will split up into all shades, producing a cavalcade of colours. It is fasci-

nating at flowering time to watch the blooms open, revealing their colours to you for the first time. This is where the true art of the plant breeder comes into play, for he must watch the plants regularly and carefully in order to decide which seedlings show signs of improvement or which may be distinct. It is in this selection work that experience and a good eye are so important. After all, it is rather pointless to spend time and effort making crosses if we are unable to recognise any improvements when the crosses mature.

Be not too hasty!

It is not wise to pass too hasty a judgement on a sweet pea seedling, for first impressions are not usually conclusive. The plants ought to be watched almost daily for weeks and closely examined to see how they react to different weather conditions and even to different light. It is also a good idea to have flowers of the best standard named varieties on hand for comparison, for few of us are able to carry colour and form in our mind's eye with any accuracy. Any plants which stand out after prolonged inspection and appear to be improvements should be labelled and their seed saved separately.

If you feel encouraged to try crossing a few sweet peas, grow the plants by the natural bush method, and not by cordon culture. The soil should err on the poorer side if possible, for plants tend to seed better with such conditions. But a word of warning, for here is a pitfall into which even Charles Unwin admitted that he fell – avoid saving too many selections, for within a very short space of time the number of selections "in the pipeline" will be confusing and embarrassing.

In the F2 generation, if a certain cross has produced a large proportion of good seedlings, it is a good idea to save this seed as a mixture from the plants which have not been labelled, for it is quite likely that in the next generation, and even in the next two or three, the cross will split up again, releasing new shades every year. The number of distinct colours which one single cross will sometimes produce can be very high. But it has to be said that generally you will find that no more than one per cent of the F2 generation have been labelled for future use.

These single plant selections from the F2s are to be sown again and kept separate. When these plants flower, the breeder will have to endure considerable disappointment, for only a small minority of the seedlings will come true to type and colour. The remainder will segregate, with wide variation in some cases.

Geese may become swans

Do not throw away these unfixed stocks, for all may not be lost. Where the level of "rogues" or wrong colours is small, pull up just these wrong plants and save the seed of about six of the remainder separately in the hope that one may prove fixed in the following year. In Charles Unwin's long experience, he was often surprised at what a large proportion of sweet pea introductions originated from stocks which were initially unfixed. Again, check the unfixed stocks daily as though they were FIs, for there may well be quite a few worth saving singly and growing on.

Admittedly, the hybridisation of sweet peas will only appeal to a few keen growers, but if you do feel encouraged to try, it is reassuring to know that it is an operation which can be performed successfully in a garden by any grower. Sweet peas were traditionally bred this way and still are. Many of the varieties which have been introduced by Unwins over the decades were bred by enthusiastic amateurs who sent their progeny for our company to trial and assess.

Unwins still welcome the opportunity to view new varieties and will offer to buy strains we consider to be improvements on those we already list.

14

A tale of woe

Much of the pace of the development of the sweet pea has been dictated by the speed of certain fortunate developments, especially colour breaks and changes of form, most notably perhaps the discovery of the "Unwin type" back in 1901.

Ninety-one years later, in the summer of 1992, a flowering plant of the elusive blue picotee was found in the company's trial grounds.

But disaster struck!

The single plant was accidentally destroyed during hoeing. The white ground sweet pea with blue edging had been discovered only three weeks earlier during a tour of the Unwins trials by a group of visitors from the National Sweet Pea Society.

Unwins director David Kerley noticed the different flower as he was guiding the guests through more than 350 different varieties.

As the genetic make-up of the plant is known to the company, it should be possible to reproduce it, although it may be up to ten years before it can be known if the characteristics of the seedling can be developed into a variety.

15

Pests and diseases of sweet peas

Sweet peas are generally trouble-free, but it is worth knowing a little about some of the problems the grower may encounter from time to time. Remember that what at first may seem like a rather long list includes several troubles which many gardeners and growers seldom if ever encounter.

If the plants are kept healthy and free from aphids (greenfly), then the chance of them contracting a disease is very small. If a plant or two starts to die, with leaves turning yellow and then brown, a soil pest at its base may be the cause, it may be leaf scorch, or one or more of the virus diseases which affect sweet peas, generally known as "streak" or "mosaic".

Leaf scorch

Not actually a disease, it is caused by the respiratory or "digestive" systems of the plant becoming unbalanced. Some varieties, especially the salmon pinks and orange shades, appear more susceptible to leaf scorch than others. Leaves of affected plants turn brittle and yellow from the bottom upwards. Flowering is not usually affected until the entire plant has been taken over. It tends to be more of a problem on light soils rather than heavy ones, and in dry seasons rather wet ones. Unfortunately, no cure is known at present and no preventative measures are known. The good news is that whilst it is found more often in the south than in the north, in

many areas it is totally unknown, and evidence sug-

gests that it is generally in decline.

Occasionally cordon-grown plants will die simply as a result of the unnatural cordon system itself. These plants are much more likely to be thrown off balance by wrong or unbalanced feeds, bad drainage or even adverse spells of weather than plants which are naturally grown. Leaf scorch and diseases rarely affect sweet peas grown in the natural, unrestricted manner, and are almost entirely confined to cordon-grown plants.

Streak and mosaic

Streak and mosaic are both virus diseases of the sweet pea, but their symptoms are markedly different from each other. With streak, the lower leaves are the first to be affected, becoming streaked with brownish-black marks and blotches. This discoloration then moves gradually up the plant.

Mosaic behaves in the opposite way. The top leaves first become veined and marbled yellow. Blooms become striped and colours tend to run. With both, the young growth at the top of the plant becomes stunted and distorted. There may be only one form of mosaic, but there are probably two or more virus diseases which we call "streak".

If the head of the plant begins to thicken and becomes stunted or malformed, it is almost certainly due to a virus disease or a very bad attack of greenfly. Plants showing any of these systems should be pulled up and burnt immediately, for they cannot be cured, and if left to grow may help spread the

Typical virus damage

infection to currently healthy plants. It is important to burn the discarded plants – do not consider composting them.

Virus diseases are usually spread among sweet pea plants by the transmission of contaminated sap by insects, almost always by greenfly. Some growers believe contaminated sap may be carried from diseased to healthy plants via knives, scissors or even fingers.

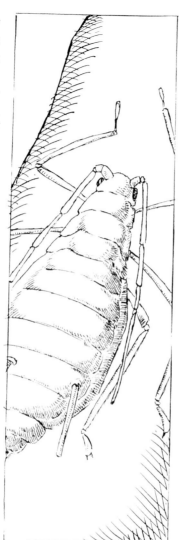

Greenfly (aphids)

Charles Unwin used to refer to the greenfly as Public Enemy Number One. At best, the greenfly saps the life out of sweet pea plants. At worst, they spread disease to a much greater extent than all the other factors put together. Their attacks are so often sly and can go unnoticed easily. As a result of this sort of delayed action effect, when a problem finally does become apparent it is sometimes attributed to a cause other than greenfly. You have been warned!

Some growers therefore take the rather extreme caution of spraying plants against greenfly throughout their life, at intervals, from the time they are about 10cm (4in) high. They do, however, desist during frosty spells. Sprayings given at intervals of around three weeks give effective protection right through the growing season.

There are many safe and effective proprietary preparations available from garden centres which are able to eliminate this pest. Whichever one you choose to use, always read the manufacturer's instructions and follow these to the letter. Remember to spray the underside of the foliage as well as the top of it. Do not wait until the plants become heavily infested, but check regularly for the first signs of colonisation. If you are also growing roses or other plants attractive to greenfly nearby, it is wise to ensure that these too remain as free as possible of the creatures.

Hibernating females and their eggs are capable of over-wintering, and as they may still be flying as late in the year as November they can therefore lay their eggs on sweet pea seedlings in the cold frame at this time. These eggs will then hatch when the weather is favourable, and begin attacking the plants at a very early stage in their growth. Sadly, it may be as late as May before it becomes apparent that the plants have been attacked and infested with virus disease. With this life cycle in mind, we can see why keen growers have such a long spraying programme against the greenfly.

Mice

These can prove a nuisance at the time of sowing seed, whether in the cold frame, greenhouse or the open ground. Traditional mousetraps are of course effective, but are not for the squeamish amongst us. I am not at all keen on poisons, especially if children, cats, dogs and wild creatures are in the vicinity, and would avoid them at all costs.

An alternative is to sprin-

kle a weak solution of Jeyes Fluid on the ground around the outside of the cold frame every two days or so. This helps keep mice away and has the advantage of masking the presence of the seed in the first place. It is worth continuing this practice for three or four weeks after seed has germinated.

I have heard that mothballs have also been used as an effective deterrent against mice if placed amongst the pots in the frame, presumably because they find the smell offensive. Old gardeners sometimes used to soak their seed in paraffin (or other equally noxious liquids) prior to sowing, but I strongly advise against this practice on environmental grounds.

Slugs and snails

A pest to all gardeners and not just sweet pea growers, they tend to attack only very young plants. There are many slug baits available from the garden centre but beware, because many are also dangerous to domestic and wild animals. Nowadays there are effective biological controls available whereby a natural predator is introduced to the pest. Many gardeners have their own favourite and sometimes bizarre means of dealing with a slug problem, ranging from the upturned half grapefruit to the "slug pub". I believe there is no substitute for picking off and destroying them as you spot them, but again this may not appeal to the weak stomached.

Pollen beetles

A tiny, black beetle about 2mm in length, which feeds on the pollen of a wide range of plants – including the sweet pea. A few years ago, it was virtually unheard of, but is now something of a plague in certain areas. This population explosion bears a strong correlation with increases in agricultural acreages put down to oilseed rape and mustard. The beetle feeds on these whilst they flower in late spring, before moving on to sweet peas, where they are a nuisance to exhibitor or cut-flower grower alike. Actual damage to the flower is minimal.

They congregate in the developing bud and in the flower keel, reducing the appeal of the blooms considerably. No single method has so far proved to be totally effective in defeating them, but if they are a problem in your area, you may like to try one of the following:

1 Place vases of cut blooms well into a dark shed or garage for a few hours, with a strong source of light beyond an open door or window. This often encourages the beetles to fly to the light. Shake the flowers afterwards to try to remove any persistent beetles.
2 Grow a small patch of yellow-flowered plants near the sweet peas to serve as a decoy crop, which can be sprayed

Pollen beetle

regularly. Rudbeckias have sometimes been used successfully for this purpose.

3 Sticky, yellow-coloured fly traps suspended nearby will attract some beetles, but can also catch 'friends' such as lacewings and ladybirds.

4 Chemical sprays are of little value as, unlike aphids, beetles do not "suck", and can only absorb through their feet.

Birds

The main problems are presented by sparrows and tits. Sparrows can play havoc with pots of seedlings whilst still in the cold frame, whilst the tits wait until around July, when they proceed to mutilate the flower buds just before they open. A light wooden framework covered with small-mesh wire netting which can be fitted over the open cold frame is very effective at keeping sparrows from feasting on the sweet pea shoots. Tits are rather more difficult to control, as they do their damage when the plants are on the point of flowering. It would appear they are attracted by the unripe pollen heads at this time, although later they may be back to open and devour the contents of any seed pods they find. All types of deterrents may be tried against tits — hawk-like and cat-like shapes, glitter-bangs, supermarket carrier bags flapping on canes to name just a few — but nothing is guaranteed to succeed. Perhaps you could take a kinder approach by offering a range of counter-attractions such as containers of peanuts, balls of seed and fat and sunflower seeds, all of which are eaten with great enthusiasm by the tits in my own garden. Very occasionally, bullfinches may cause damage by eating the base of the blooms, but to perfectly honest I would be so delighted to see a bullfinch in my garden that it is a price I would be prepared to pay. Pigeons, too, can sometimes be a nuisance, but the good old scarecrow is usually a sufficient deterrent if they are a problem in your area. Special nylon line which hums in a breeze when pulled taut is also effective against pigeons.

Wireworms and other soil pests

Wireworms are brownish-yellow, up to 2.5cm (1in) long, quite hard to the touch and thin. They can damage plants by burrowing into the stem just below soil level. The old remedy of the potato or carrot trap is usually able to deal with this pest. This consists of a piece of carrot or potato stuck on sticks and buried about 5cm (2in) below the surface of the soil in positions where wireworms are suspected. These should then be checked every day so that any wireworms embedded in them can be destroyed

Cockchafer grubs are sometimes the cause of a plant suddenly wilting for no obvious reason. They bite through the stem just below ground level. If this happens to a plant, check the soil close by for these soft, yellowy grubs with distinctive brown heads, usually about 2.5cm (1in) long and usually curled up. Similarly, leatherjackets (the larvae of the Daddy Longlegs) are brown, 2.5cm (1in) long grubs which also damage plant stems just below the level of the soil. Colonies of woodlice are sometimes attracted to old wooden cold frames, and may damage the shoots of seedlings shortly after germination. All the above can be effectively dealt with by the use of chemical preparations obtainable from garden centres if desired.

Bud drop

Bud drop is not actually a disease, but is rather an annoying phase which usually passes fairly quickly. It is mainly a problem just as the plants begin to bloom, often when conditions are cool and damp. Some or all of the buds may turn yellow and drop off before opening, usually when quite small. No one really knows exactly what causes this condition, but too much moisture at the roots, over-watering, over-feeding, insufficient sun and warmth and abnormally cold or variable weather are all felt to be factors, either singly or combined. There is very little which can be done other than waiting for it to pass, except perhaps to withhold watering and feeding for its duration.

Cordon-grown plants are much more liable to bud drop than those grown naturally – extremely annoying to the exhibitor if it happens just before a show! There is a body of opinion which says some varieties are more susceptible to bud drop than others, and that modern varieties are more so than older ones. This has not been proven, and the pattern of behaviour of different varieties is irregular and unpredictable, varying both from garden to garden and from season to season.

Blindness

On cordon-grown plants a leader will occasionally just peter out and come to a dead end. If this happens, a side shoot should be used to take its place. Newcomers to cordon growing can sometimes find they have pinched out the last remaining side shoot before they realise the plant is going blind, but experience will soon help the grower realise the increasingly thin appearance of a leader in good time. The cause of this blindness is still not understood, although it is quite likely due to a check in growth – perhaps frost action – sustained much earlier than when the blindness actually occurs. If blindness occurs in naturally grown plants it presents no problems as new growth will rapidly replace any that may fizzle out. The last thing I wish to do is to discourage people from growing sweet peas, indeed quite the reverse is true. So do not begin to think that your growing will be beset by the above pests and diseases in turn, each queuing up to have a go at your plants. In practice, few troubles are seen by most people. Balance all this against the fact that when all is said and done sweet peas are hardy annuals, the most trouble-free group of all plants.

Blindness following frosts

16

Unwins sweet peas and the New Zealand connection

Sweet pea seed is produced commercially in a wide range of areas around the world, including the United States, Eastern Europe, Malta and Continental Europe, although little is now grown in Great Britain.

Little did Charles Unwin realise as he set out to visit his daughter Patricia in New Zealand in 1958 that between them they would revolutionise the production of sweet pea seed to the benefit of all gardeners.

The favourable New Zealand climate coupled with the six months seasonal difference

An Unwins seed crop growing in New Zealand

Pat and Bridget Richardson assess the crop

Hand sorting – any sub-standard seeds are rejected

Unwins staff hand sort around 45,000,000 seeds annually

from Britain meant that seed of new varieties harvested at Unwins' Histon trial grounds in August could be sent to New Zealand for immediate sowing, as that country's spring begins in September. With the resultant seed crop harvestable in February, New Zealand's autumn, Charles appreciated the value of having two crops in one year – invaluable for the faster introduction of new varieties. Seed could then be returned to Britain for packeting, for sowing by gardeners the following autumn.

He persuaded Patricia to start producing sweet pea seed crops, and so a link was established between the two branches of the family which continues to this day because the operation is so successful. This New Zealand-produced seed soon established an excellent reputation amongst Unwins customers, and is generally regarded to be the best available anywhere in the world.

Every operation from sowing, through "roguing" (the elimination of off-types) to harvesting and sorting is performed by hand. Seed is hand-picked into an apron-pouch and

emptied into clearly labelled sacks supported by metal tripods. Harvesting generally takes between six and eight weeks.

On arrival at Unwins' premises in Britain, the seeds are then tested for vigour and their powers of germination in the company's seed testing laboratory, prior to packeting.

Each sweet pea seed is inspected visually and hand-picked by a member of staff to ensure only seeds of the highest quality are packeted. All shrivelled, wrinkled or cracked seeds are rejected. Around 45,000,000 sweet pea seeds are checked by this method every year. It is admittedly a labour-intensive operation, but ensures our reputation as sweet pea seedsmen remains as high as possible.

Unwins maintain an extensive breeding programme of sweet peas, and have an annual trial of sweet peas, which we believe to be the biggest in the world. It is part of the company's continued commitment to the flower which helped to found the company back in 1903.

17

The sweet pea hall of fame

So many people have contributed to the development and popularity of the sweet pea over the years that in singling out a few for special mention, many are not named. It is unfortunate but inevitable in a volume of this size. I hope readers will agree the following must all be included in the "Hall of Fame".

Franciscus Cupani

The Sicilian monk who is credited with sending the first sweet pea seeds to England. They were sent in 1699 to Dr Robert Uvedale of Enfield.

Henry Eckford

Rightly referred to as the Father of the Sweet Pea for the pioneering work he did on the grandiflora sweet peas at Wem in Shropshire during the Victorian era. He took a rather ordinary little flower and transformed it into something which caught the public imagination as the forerunner of all our modern-day types.

Charles Unwin, a leading authority

William Unwin

He had the good fortune to be "visited" by a chance mutation of the variety Prima Donna back in 1901, and the good sense to realise what an advance he had witnessed. He was able to transfer the desirable characteristics of this mutation to other colours of sweet pea, and on the strength of this founded the company W. J. Unwin Ltd, now known as Unwins Seeds.

Ken Colledge

Mrs Bernard Jones

Charles Unwin

Son of William and probably the leading authority on sweet peas of the twentieth century. Sweet peas became his passion and over many decades he bred a host of new varieties including Frances Perry, Andrew Unwin, Champagne Bubbles and Monarch's Diamond. He died in 1986.

Revd Ken Colledge

The Revd Colledge spent much of his time hybridising and developing sweet peas until his death in 1990. His two best-known varieties are the legendary Leamington and Southbourne, and he also bred Terry Wogan, Royal Baby, Diamond Wedding, Nancy Colledge and Charles Unwin.

Bernard Jones

One of the outstanding exhibitors of his time and an acknowledged expert on sweet peas, Bernard Jones died in January 1996. His remarkable breeding achievements include Alice Hardwicke, White Supreme, Brian Clough, The Doctor, Red Arrow and Mrs Bernard Jones.

David Lemon

Mr Lemon worked for many years as a breeder with American seed companies. He is responsible for breeding the Jet Set, Mammoth and Supersnoop series.

Jim Tandy

The breeder of the tendril-free Snoopea, working for E .W. King of Kelvedon, Essex.

Keith Hammett

The New Zealand-based breeder of a beautiful race of bicolor sweet peas described in the chapter entitled *Classification of Sweet Peas*. Much of his hybridisation work involves old-fashioned types and *Lathyrus* species in the search for the elusive yellow sweet pea.

Robert Bolton and Tom Bolton

Robert Bolton founded his company in 1901 at Warton in Lancashire, but it has now been based at Birdbrook, Essex, for many years and remains family owned. The business was carried on by Tom Bolton, and his son, Robert, now heads this firm of sweet pea specialists. Among their famous introductions are Elizabeth Taylor, Mrs R. Bolton and Southampton.

William and Anton Zvolanek

American specialists in the earlier decades of the twentieth century. They raised the Butterfly sweet peas, a new race with narrow petals, which created an impression of great lightness and daintiness. The Zvolaneks were also responsible for much of the early work which was conducted in developing multi-blooms.

18

Sweet peas around the world

We know the sweet pea came from Sicily to England, but that it probably originated in Malta, where it still grows wild. That it is regarded as such a British flower nowadays is no doubt due to the huge following it enjoys in the United Kingdom amongst gardeners and exhibitors alike.

Looking further afield, gardeners in Germany and Eastern European countries are keen growers, particularly of the Cuthbertson floribunda types. I have met avid sweet pea growers in both Russia and Latvia who manage to produce superb blooms in an often inhospitable climate.

Sweden buys and grows many packets of seed per person, while the Netherlands has its own sweet pea society which stages an annual exhibition supported by Her Royal Highness Princess Juliana.

While New Zealand produces much sweet pea seed, a great amount is also produced in California. Sweet peas are grown as an early spring crop as the plants soon become burnt up by the hot summers of the west coast. But it is in the northwestern states such as Washington and Oregon where sweet peas are popular with American gardeners. The cool maritime climate of these states provides a long flowering season for the plants.

Sweet pea seeds are available by mail order in the following countries from:

THE NETHERLANDS
Hortiprom
Convent 9
1613 EM Grootebroek
Netherlands

(suppliers of Unwins sweet pea seeds in 1996)

UNITED STATES OF AMERICA
W. Atlee Burpee & Co
Warminster PA 18974

Park Seed
Cokesbury Road
Greenwood
SC 29647

NEW ZEALAND

Kings Herbs Ltd
PO Box 19-084
Avondale
Auckland

AUSTRALIA

Kings Herb Seeds
PO Box 975
Penrith
NSW 2751

19

Unwins sweet peas introduced since 1911

1911   Mrs W J Unwin, Nettie Jenkins, Eric Harvey, May Farquhar, Freda Unwin, Mrs H D Tigwell, Mrs R Hallam, Madge Ridgard

1912   Walter P Wright, Leslie Imber, Winifred Unwin, Cyril Unwin

1913   Mrs D Denholm Fraser, Muriel Quick, Victor Unwin, Dora Hopley, The Abbott

1914   Phyllis, Zillah Smith, Edith King, Mabel Baccus, May Unwin

1915   Edward Cowdy, Mrs J Balmer

1916   Mrs Arthur Stevenson

1917   Unwin's Lavender, Unwin's Cream

1918   The Queen, Betty

1919   Mrs J T Wakefield

1920   Unwins Pink, Twilight

1921   Gladys, Royal Scot, Picture

1922   Unwins Crimson, Edith, Captain Charles Burgess

1923   May Cowdy, Mrs H Richards, Hawlmark Pink Improved, Improved Mrs J T Wakefield

1924   W J Unwin, Mrs Chas W J Unwin, Improved Faerie Queen, Improved Conquest

1925   Mauve Beauty, Lady Gay, Blue Butterfly

1926   Queen of Roumania, Wistaria, Sybil Henshaw, Mrs Horace Wright, Twinkles

1927   Chieftain, Model, Gleneagles, Del Monte, Lilac Queen, What Joy

1928	Dainty Lady, Pink Tip, Jessie Collingridge, Harlequin, Victoria	1949	Autumn Gold, Harmony, Lilacea, Blue Ice
1929	Blue Bell, Charm, Elizabeth, Ascot, Flamingo, Idyl	1950	Unwins Salmon Shades, Moonlight, Albatross, June Rose
1930	Clematis, Satin, Mauve, Columbine	1951	Betty Felicity, Pink Opal, Elizabeth Taylor
1931	Innocence, Blue Wings, The Clown, Fantasy, Coquette	1952	Myosotis, Pixie, Leicester, Brightling
1932	Marion, Scarlet Flame, Pink Gem, Rosie, Salmon Glow	1953	Twink, Coquette, Jester, Petunia
1933	Lilac Domino, Red Beacon, Pierrot	1954	Edith, Red Velvet
1934	Rosemary, Electra, Gloria	1955	Mrs Tyndale, Artiste, Black Velvet, Satin Glow
1935	Patricia Unwin	1956	Rosy Frills, Joyce, Fairy
1936	Melody, Delice, Exquisite	1957	Midnight, Rapture, Classic, Red Pepper
1937	Snowdon, Betty, Vivid, Winsome	1958	Ivory Prince, Rose Fondant
1938	Discovery, King Lavender, Ruffled Sparkle	1960	Ballerina, Patience, Evensong, Sheila Jean
1939	Leader, Vista, Autocrat, Rarity	1961	Vogue, Winsome, Red Admiral
1940	Crimson, Emblem, Glamour, Viola, Rosea, Minuet, Improved Pat	1962	Snocap, Carnival, Bouquet, Nocturne
1941	Spitfire, Joan	1963	Lavender Lace, Royalty, Pink Magic, Flare
1948	Radiant, Purple Velvet, Roselight, Anchusa	1964	Pastel, Spotlight, Brocade, Sonata

1965	Mischief, Blue Veil, Melodie, Dearest	1978	Rhapsody, Unique, Polly Willson, Flirt
1966	Cheripink, Saturn, Poppet, Caress	1979	Beacon, White Ruffles, The Doctor, Lustre
1967	Delice, Carousel, Sun Dance, Cherie	1980	Diamond Wedding, Sheila Macqueen, Nancy Colledge, Fiona
1968	Fair Lady, Firefly, Hunter's Moon, Modesty	1981	Ascot, Frances Perry, Mrs Bernard Jones, Blue Danube
1969	Sweetheart, Signal, Legend, Xtasy	1982	Royal Wedding, Brian Clough, Pat Mitchell, Cream Southbourne
1970	Sally Patricia, Duchess of Bedford, Reward, Blue Rinse	1983	Royal Baby, Terry Wogan, Red Arrow, Lady Fairbairn
1971	Milestone, Blue Riband, Blue Frost, Radiance	1984	Our Joyce, Duchess of Roxburghe, Cyril Fletcher, Gypsy Rose
1972	Sunset, Cream Ruffles, White Leamington, Blue Velvet	1985	Diana, Charles Unwin, Catherine
1973	Embers, Opal, Southbourne, Royalist	1986	Midnight, Dynasty, Champagne Bubbles, Pink Bouquet
1974	Red Beacon, Fairytale, Peerless Pink, Blaze	1987	Colin Unwin, Band Aid, Can-Can, Monarch's Diamond
1975	Eclipse, Artiste, Caprice, Black Prince	1988	Alastair, Jilly, Cambridge Blue
1976	Old Times, Fancy Free, Topscore, Sunsilk	1989	Steve Davis, Andrew Unwin, Fatima
1977	Salmon Frills, Whisper, Blue Mantle, Sally Unwin	1990	Vera Lynn, Pink Expression, Charlie's Angel

1991	Queen Mother, Candy, Fergus	1995	Princess Juliana, Thomas Bradley, Rosanna Alice
1992	Rosalind, Camilla, Ken Colledge	1996	Mars, Nimbus, Bridget, Macmillan Nurse
1993	Columbus, Her Majesty, Daphne		
1994	Arthur Hellyer, W J Unwin, Edward Unwin		

Company transport between the wars

The National Sweet Pea Society

As your interest in sweet peas grows (and I hope this volume has encouraged you!), you may consider joining the National Sweet Pea Society (NSPS). Founded in 1901, the same year as the appearance of both Gladys Unwin and Countess Spencer, the Society encourages the cultivation and improvement of the species.

Each year it holds at least two exhibitions where its cups and awards are keenly contested. It also conducts annual trials of newly raised seedlings. These are grown in conjunction with the Royal Horticultural Society at their Wisley, Surrey, Gardens, and judged by a joint committee of both Societies. Trials are also held each year by the Scottish National Sweet Pea, Rose and Carnation Society.

The National Sweet Pea Society publishes its Sweet Pea Annual, a volume containing a great amount of information essential to all lovers of the flower. Bulletins on topics of interest are also issued regularly. The Society offers the opportunity at shows, meetings and other gatherings to meet other members. The country is covered by a number of District Representatives who organise lectures and other events for members in their own area.

Details of membership may be obtained from the following:

Mr J R F Bishop
Hon. Secretary NSPS
3 Chalk Farm Road
Stokenchurch
High Wycombe
Buckinghamshire HP14 3TB

and for the Scottish Society from:

Mrs J Reid
Gen. Secretary SNSPRCS
72 West George Street
Coatbridge ML5 2DD

(Details correct as at March 1996)